Contents

2 Director's Foreword
3 Sponsor's Foreword
4 The Prizes
5 The Judges

Schweppes Prize
6 First Shara Henderson
8 Second Philipp Ebeling
10 Third Ric Bower
12 Fourth Magnus Reed

Deloitte Award
14 Winner Karoline Hjorth

16 Exhibitors

Director's Foreword

What makes a portrait special? What makes it stand out from the images around it? What attracts us to spend time considering the face of someone that we do not know and have not met? How does a great portrait capture a certain look, a smile, a frown (or even, in the case of photography, an indifferent response to the camera), making it the centre of what catches our eye, and starting the process of making it a visual memory?

As the 6,000 submitted portraits – faces, heads and figures – jostle for the attention of the jury, the answer to these questions is entirely practical. The comparisons are immediate and telling, and the less striking images gradually fall away from consideration. The photographs are judged anonymously – the jury knows nothing of each photographer. Their selection is not really a question of a particular style or technique (although both of these things matter), but the importance of conveying something of the period we live in, how we see each other, and how we are prepared to be seen. Perversely, those that appear as the most timeless portraits, may also seem the most contemporary. Equally, although there is nothing innately virtuous in the offbeat or the haphazard, the perfect technical photographic portrait is not always the one that attracts greatest interest or discussion.

Only sixty photographs can be included and the selection of these is a process of great debate. Members of the jury argue for different works, and over two days divergent or convergent priorities and interests emerge. I hope that the many and various qualities of the selected works will interest and engage you as much as they excited us.

I should like to acknowledge and thank all of the many photographers from around the world who submitted to the 2005 *Schweppes* Photographic Portrait Prize. Many congratulations go to this year's winners: Shara Henderson, Philipp Ebeling, Ric Bower and Magnus Reed, and to Karoline Hjorth, winner of the 2005 Deloitte Award. This is awarded to a portrait photographer aged twenty-five or under and represents the continuing success of the Gallery's partnership with Deloitte, whose support for commissions, contemporary displays and touring is making a positive difference to the Gallery's work.

I want to thank Coca-Cola Great Britain as the overall sponsors of the Prize and the exhibition. Their support makes possible an important opportunity for the wider recognition of the best images that are being created in the dynamic field of photographic portraiture.

I should like to thank my fellow judges: Eamonn McCabe, Terence Pepper, Julia Peyton-Jones and Val Williams. They worked hard across two long days and were passionate and determined in their choices. My thanks also go to the staff of the National Portrait Gallery, particularly Pim Baxter, Naomi Conway, Neil Evans, Susie Foster, Clare Freestone, John Haywood, Helen James, Beatrice Hosegood, Ruth Müller-Wirth, Howard Smith, Kathleen Soriano, Rosie Wilson and especially Sarah Wang, as well as the designers NB: Studio, and the interviewer Richard McClure, for all their hard work on the exhibition and this catalogue.

Sandy Nairne, Director,
National Portrait Gallery

Sponsor's Foreword

Now in its third year, the *Schweppes* Photographic Portrait Prize showcases the very best of today's portrait photography in a way that is guaranteed to provoke curiosity, delight, discussion and enjoyment.

As a brand with over 200 year's heritage, experience, and a strong association with creativity, *Schweppes* believes in the power of the arts to bring people together – promoting lively debate and interaction.

We are proud to sponsor the 2005 *Schweppes* Photographic Portrait Prize, allowing fresh talent a unique platform to inspire and challenge us with images that reveal a fascinating perspective on the diverse and beguiling nature of the human spirit.

We hope you enjoy the exhibition.

Charlotte Oades, President,
Coca-Cola Great Britain

The Prizes

Schweppes Photographic Portrait Prize

The *Schweppes* Photographic Portrait Prize is open to photographers from around the world aged eighteen or over.

The first prize winner is Shara Henderson, who receives £12,000

The second prize winner is Philipp Ebeling, who receives £3,000

The third prize winner is Ric Bower, who receives £2,000

The fourth prize winner is Magnus Reed, who receives £1,000

Deloitte Award

The Deloitte Award is for the best portrait taken by a photographer aged twenty-five or under. The Award forms one part of a larger contemporary photography-based partnership between Deloitte and the National Portrait Gallery, which started in autumn 2003. Deloitte is supporting several areas within the Gallery's ground-floor contemporary photographic displays, as well as donating an acquisition fund for photographic portraits of figures from public life, and helping the Gallery to develop its UK touring programme of contemporary photography from the Collection.

The winner is Karoline Hjorth, who receives £5,000

If you would like to join the mailing list to receive an entry form for next year's Photographic Portrait Prize, please send your full contact details to:

Photographic Portrait Prize 2006
Marketing Department
National Portrait Gallery
St Martin's Place
London WC2H 0HE

The Judges

Chair: Sandy Nairne, Director, National Portrait Gallery
'This year's judging involved an exhilarating toing and froing between careful consideration and close debate, starting with the 6,000 images and gradually whittling them down to the sixty superb portraits selected for the exhibition. And then there was further close examination to find the most worthy winners of the prizes. As there are more good portraits than prizes to go round, this was the hardest part of the process.'

Julia Peyton-Jones, Director, Serpentine Gallery
'This Award involved looking at 6,000 photographs. The sheer diversity of the images was remarkable and over two days the judges had an opportunity to see a wealth of talent from all over the world. The discussion amongst us was fascinating as well as stimulating. The focus on what we saw was intense and I learned about photographic portraits through the eyes of the rest of the group. I could not be more pleased to have been a judge of this year's Award.'

Val Williams, Curator, Writer and Director of Research, Centre for Photography and the Archive, University of the Arts London
'Judging the *Schweppes* Portrait Prize is a remarkable experience. The number and variety of photographs submitted demonstrates the range of practices within photography, the extent of its subject matter and the breadth of what photographers perceive to be "portraiture". All of the photographers who submit to the Prize do so anonymously, so one confronts these pictures without any context of the photographers' reputations, nationalities or ages. Refreshingly, the photographs assume lives of their own – become simply images. From studio-based portraits clearly made by photographers at a high technical and aesthetic level to lovingly crafted portraits of friends and family (and sometimes a combination of both), the submission shows that we are all committed to the photographic portrait – its ability to still time and capture memory. The photographs selected for the final exhibition all have something special and out of the ordinary – public figures perhaps caught off guard by the knowing gaze of a professional portraitist, a child in a red dress, a salesman in a carpet shop, a lively family still for the occasion.'

Eamonn McCabe, Photographer, the *Guardian*
'I was delighted to be asked to be a judge of this year's *Schweppes* competition. Although just looking at 6,000 photographs is pretty daunting, let alone choosing a winner. But what I really wanted to find out was why a certain type of picture usually won. As a photographer of famous people (I've even got some photographs in the National Portrait Gallery's collection), I have entered the competition for years, but never had a photograph chosen for the exhibition. Now I know why – the standard is so high, I haven't got a chance!'

Terence Pepper, Curator of Photographs, National Portrait Gallery
'Each year the standard of entries remains remarkably high and this year it was as heartbreaking as ever to have to agree to select only sixty photographs from so many others that were almost equally insightful, moving and excellent in all the ways that a good portrait can be.'

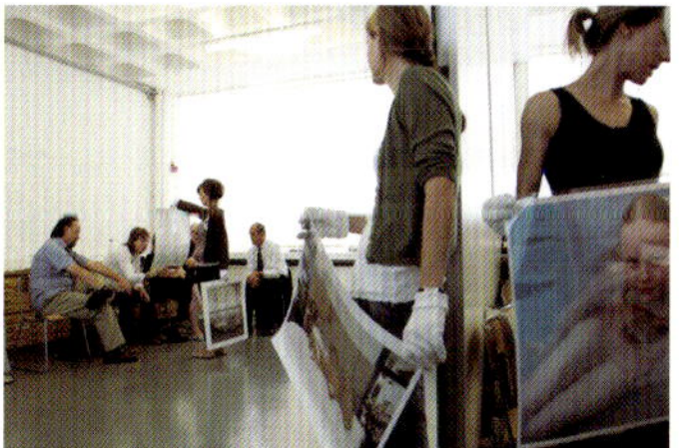

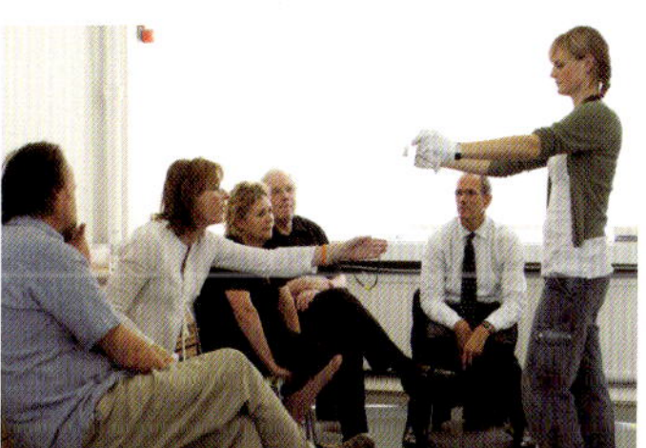

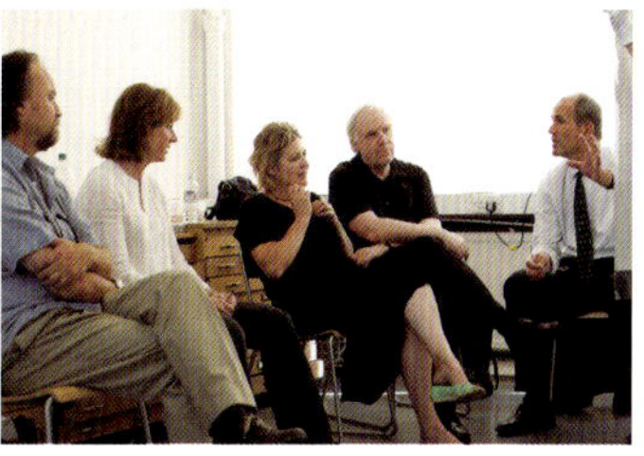

Schweppes First Prize Winner Shara Henderson

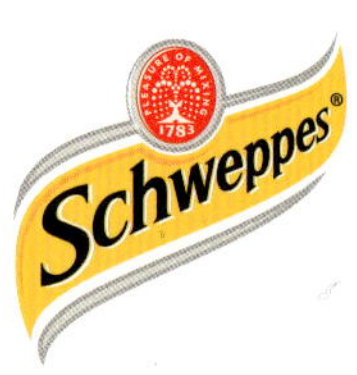

Visiting her Polish-born partner's family in the industrial town of Brzeg Dolny in the summer of 2004, Australian photographer Shara Henderson used the trip as an opportunity to capture some new additions to her portfolio. Asking a young acquaintance to round up the local kids for a spur-of-the-moment shoot, she spent a few hours photographing the children as they played in the neighbourhood. Her winning entry in this year's *Schweppes* Photographic Portrait Prize, *Girl With Baby – Poland*, is a result of the impromptu session.

'The girl in the portrait, Agnieszka, was one of the quieter ones. She just sat in the background and didn't play up to the camera,' says 27-year-old Henderson. 'I turned around and saw her holding the baby, Dominika, and thought it would make the perfect photograph. I carefully repositioned them without changing too much as I like to keep things as natural as possible. My style is documentary in a sense as I like to capture real people in real situations, but it's not as if I run around snapping. Every photograph I take is thought-out and composed. I use a tripod and everything is quite structured.'

Photographing children has become Henderson's foremost activity since she began 'dabbling' with a camera in high school. 'I'd take portraits of children all day long if I could. They tend to be far less guarded than adults and give you a lot more,' she says. 'Because of the language barrier, I didn't really communicate with Agnieszka so I don't know much about her. But I was drawn to the strength of character that radiated from her face. Some people who view the portrait believe she's the baby's mother. She's not, but I don't mind the resulting ambiguity.'

Graduating with a BA in Photography from the Royal Melbourne Institute of Technology in 2003, Henderson then spent three months in New York as an intern to Mary Ellen Mark. Besides the more mundane duties of cataloguing the photographer's vast archive at her SoHo studio, Henderson also assisted Mark on a number of photo shoots, including the 2004 anti-war demonstrations in Manhattan.

'She's a very interesting lady. I've always loved her work, so it was a great experience. She's influenced my methods greatly, as have Richard Avedon and Steve McCurry. Most of my portraits are taken in a similar vein to Mark, wandering unscheduled around the streets with my Mamiya, approaching and shooting subjects spontaneously.'

Displaying typically Australian wanderlust, Henderson landed in London last year with just £200 in her pocket. She soon found employment running a photographic studio in Docklands, and is currently moving towards a career as a freelance photographer. 'My aim is to shoot things that excite me – anything from advertising campaigns to magazine covers. I love to make everyday situations beautiful, to show a side that many people do not see, or happen to overlook.'

Interviewed by
Richard McClure

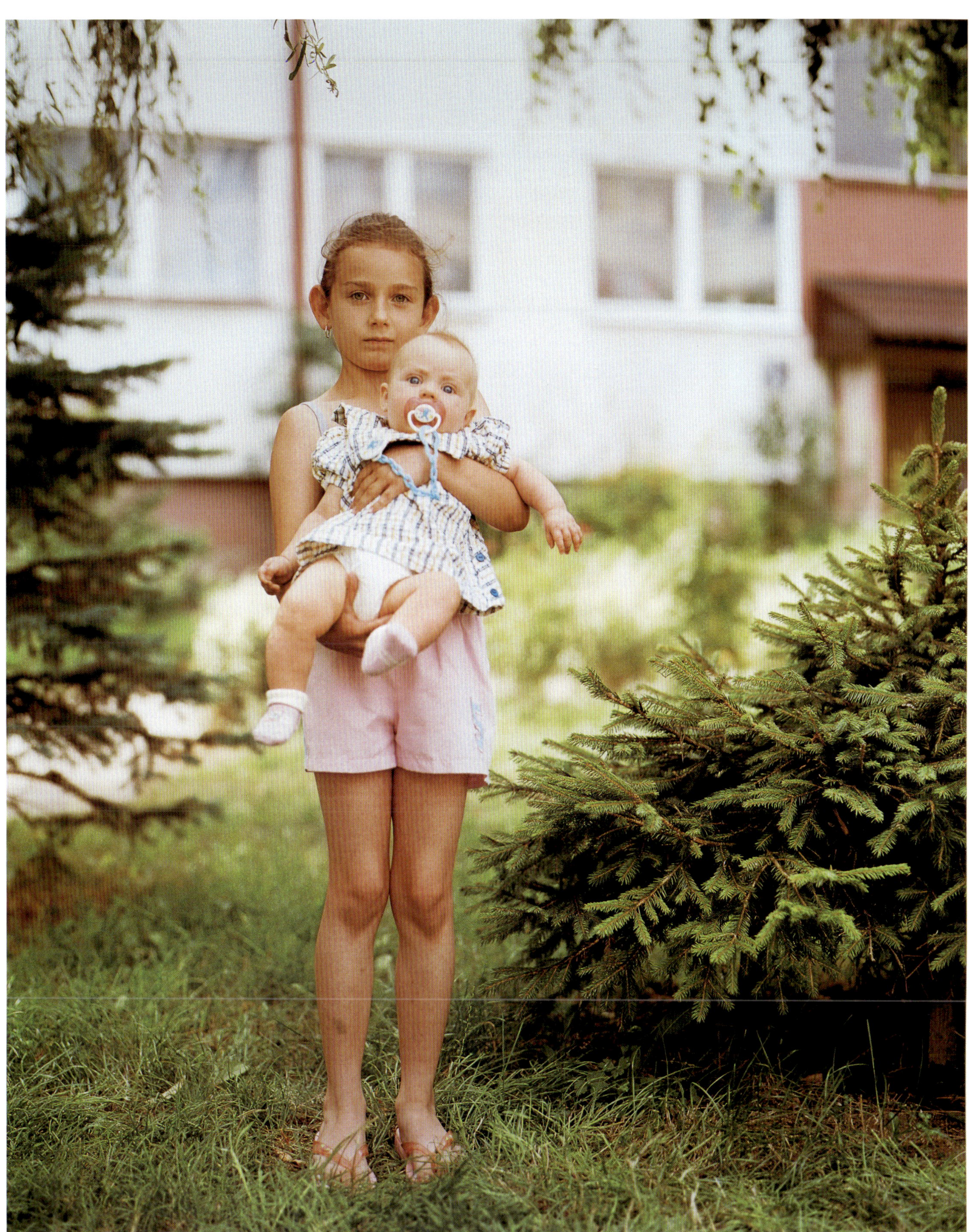

Schweppes Second Prize Winner Philipp Ebeling

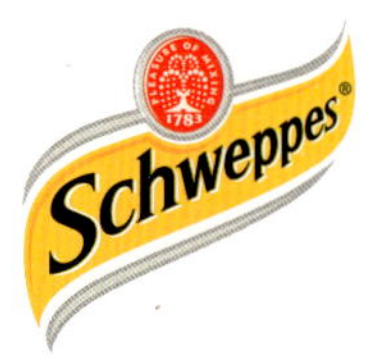

A long-standing contributor to *Dazed & Confused*, German-born photographer Philipp Ebeling shot his *Schweppes* entry, *Georgina, Royal College of Art, London*, at the style magazine's re:creation awards, an annual event to honour the UK's finest young creative talent. Commissioned to photograph the prizewinners, Ebeling saw immediately that his portrait of 21-year-old illustrator Georgina Portier was 'a cut above the rest'. Born with multiple cysts that affected the functioning of her kidneys, Portier had her left kidney removed when she was only four months old, followed by a transplant of her remaining kidney at the age of seven. She received her award for designing a poster to encourage more people to be organ donors.

'Georgina had been in a life-or-death situation as a child, but I wasn't aware of her medical history when I took the photograph,' says 28-year-old Ebeling. 'Ideally, I would have liked more information about her, but that's the mystery of photography. You can still produce a strong image while knowing nothing about your subject. Georgina has an extraordinary face and she bought that great outfit especially for the ceremony. You can tell she was over the moon to win the award.'

Leaving his home town Hanover for London eight years ago, Ebeling ditched thoughts of becoming a doctor to take a BA in Photography at the London College of Printing (now the London College of Communication). Since then, he has established himself as one of the UK's leading young photographers. Besides his work for *Dazed & Confused*, he regularly shoots cover portraits for *Time Out*. Working with a Pentax 6x7, his recent subjects include rock bands Coldplay and Franz Ferdinand, film director Lars von Trier and Prime Minister Tony Blair – 'one of the most media-savvy people you'll ever meet'.

Ebeling's *Schweppes* success follows his first prize in last year's *Observer* Hodge Photographic Award, achieved with his series *10 Minutes One January Afternoon in Whitechapel*, which he took during a snowstorm outside his East End flat. 'I'd always wanted to photograph Whitechapel market as it's right on my doorstep, but I needed the right occasion,' he explains. 'One night, I got home during a blizzard, rushed upstairs to get my camera and shot a roll of film. That's how I usually work, both in portraiture and landscape. I'm more an observing kind of photographer, rather than creating a scene like Jeff Wall or being opinionated like Martin Parr. I admire what they do but I have a different way of seeing.'

Currently living in Treviso, Italy, after receiving a scholarship from Fabrica, the Benetton artistic research foundation, Ebeling is due to begin a project that examines issues of European identity. 'I've always been interested in the concept of Europe – what we have in common and what we don't. Although I was born in Germany, I'm very much an English photographer. It was London's urban social texture that inspired me to pick up a camera in the first place.'

Interviewed by Richard McClure

Philipp Ebeling

Georgina, Royal College of Art, London March 2004

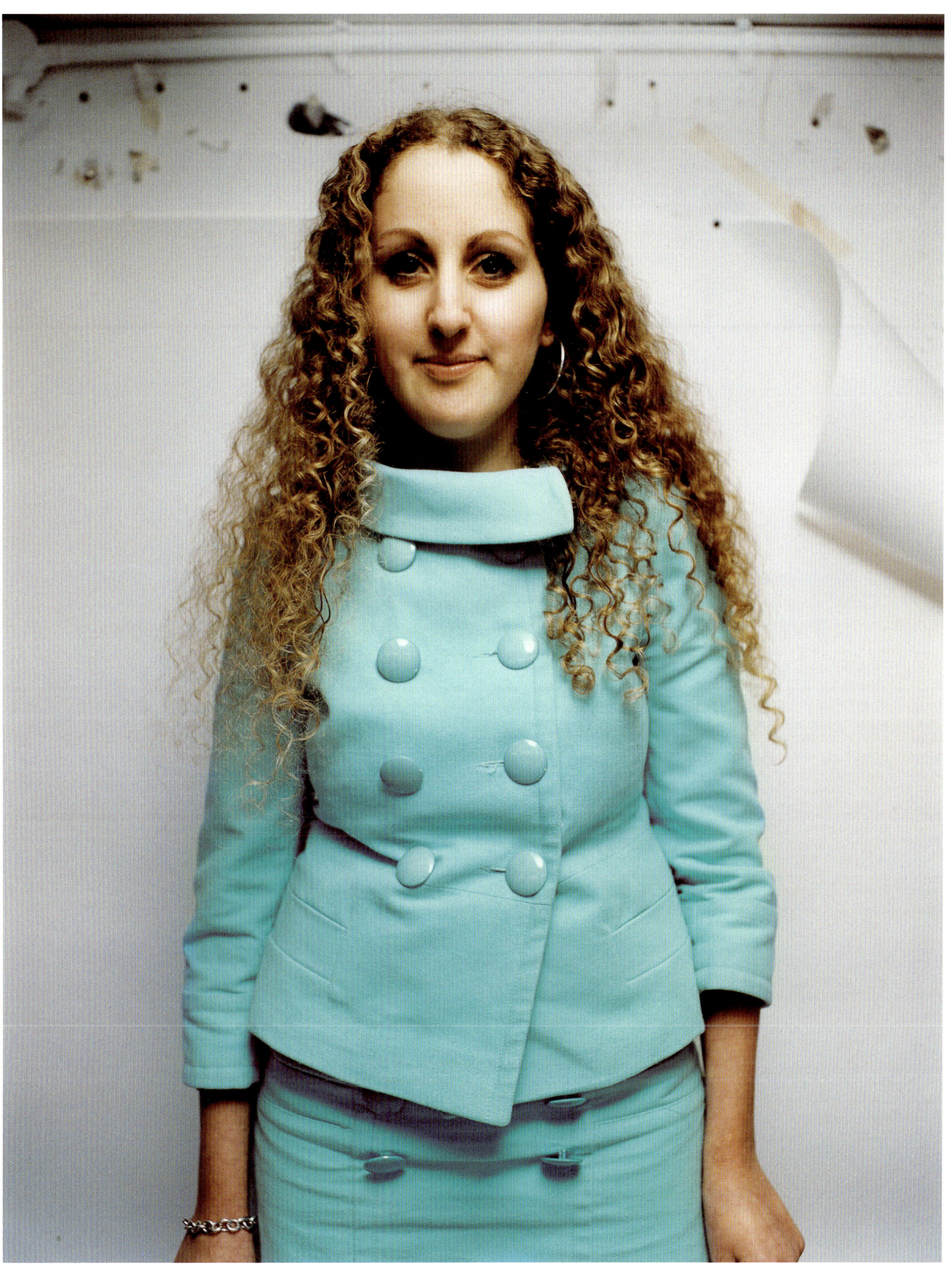

Schweppes Third Prize Winner Ric Bower

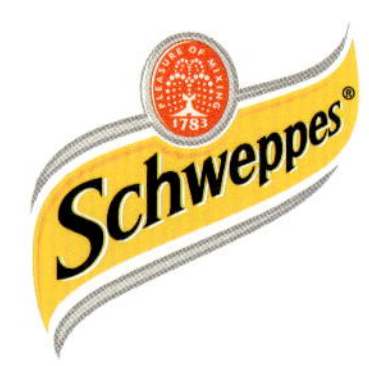

Like much of Ric Bower's painting and photography, his *Schweppes* entry, *Three Generations*, is rooted in his firmly held religious beliefs as a born-again Christian. Graduating this year with a first-class BA (Hons) in Photography from Coleg Sir Gar in Carmarthen, Wales, Bower took the portrait as part of his degree show – one of a number of images exploring the subject of prayer. The photograph shows his wife Share, daughters Jasmin and Amber, and mother-in-law Mary during a Christian get-together to celebrate spring harvest at a holiday camp in Minehead.

'I spend a lot of time in prayer and the idea for the series came to me while I was actually praying,' says 37-year-old Bower. 'The portrait is about the transference of faith down the generations; the corridor of lights in the image alludes to the passing of time. There's a misconception among some Christians that once you accept Jesus into your heart, life will be trouble-free. But my wife has wrestled with issues of faith and no doubt my children will do the same one day. I wanted to create a tension, an uneasiness, that suggests this struggle.'

Brought up in Hampshire, Bower came to God after developing a 'horrendous drug problem' in his late teens. Moving to Spain for five months, where he became a pavement artist, he returned to the UK and graduated with a BA in Fine Art from Manchester Polytechnic in 1992, then lived as a New Age traveller for several years, continuing to make his living by copying the Old Masters onto pavements around the country. Now settled in Wales, he combines commercial camera work with painting, drawing and teaching. Earlier this year, he was commissioned by Cardiff's National Museum and Gallery to photograph writer Sarah Waters for its permanent collection.

Drawing upon such diverse influences as Caravaggio and US photographer Gregory Crewdson for *Three Generations*, Bower carefully positioned his family members beneath a strip lamp to create a 'conceptual tableaux', shooting the scene with a full-frame Canon digital. 'There's a long tradition of light being used as a symbol for the supernatural involvement of God in Christian imagery, but I wanted to infuse it with the accessibility of a household object. I'm becoming increasingly interested in engineering my photographs. It is the antithesis of the "decisive moment" but, as a painter, it's an approach I'm comfortable with.'

With Bower's faith acting as the 'primary informer' of all his work, he hopes the *Prayer* series will counter Magnum photographer Carl de Keyzer's well-known series, *God Inc.*, which depicts the extremities of Christian fundamentalism in the USA. '*God Inc.* has had a profound effect on me, partly because of the brilliance of de Keyzer's perception and partly for the discomfort that I feel being lumped in as a Christian with the lunacy he portrays. *Prayer* was motivated by a desire to counter the conclusions he invites his viewers to draw. Evangelising is a central part of what I do in my work. My job is to be faithful to God and Jesus.'

Interviewed by
Richard McClure

Ric Bower

Three Generations
from the series
Prayer
April 2005

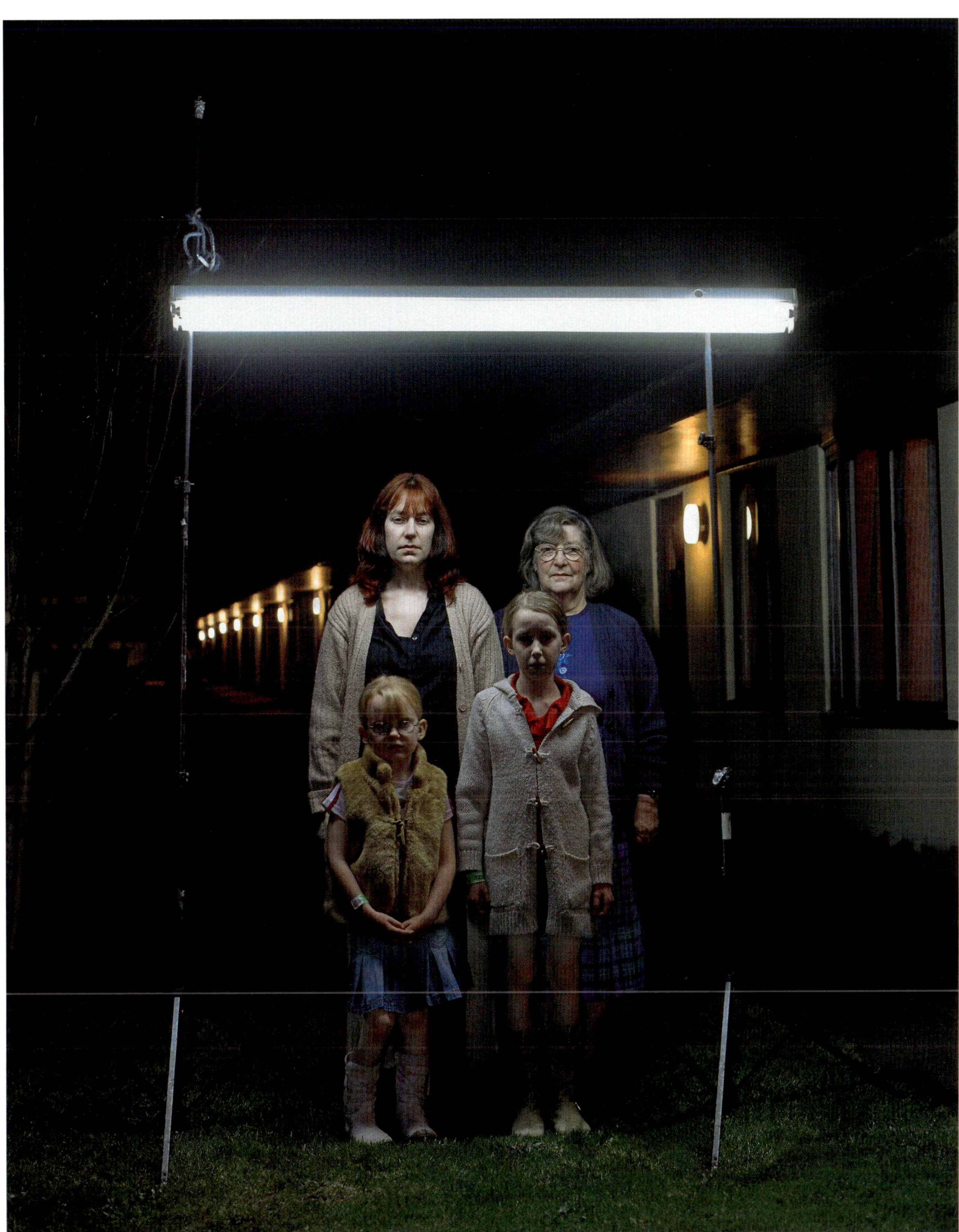

Schweppes Fourth Prize Winner Magnus Reed

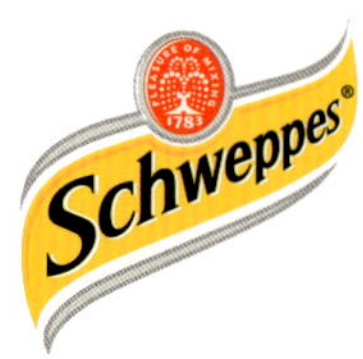

Magnus Reed was stuck in a dead-end job at a Stockholm hotel when a conversation with an Afghan colleague prompted him to quit work to pursue his growing interest in photography. Aged twenty-one, he travelled to Afghanistan where he spent two months documenting the brutal fighting between Mujahadeen guerillas and the invading Russian army. Although the experience reinforced his desire to make a living from his lens, he quickly realised that war photography was not for him.

'Afghanistan was a very harsh awakening. It was addictive and dangerous,' he recalls. 'I was extremely lucky – I could have died about four times. At the time, I thought I wanted to do that kind of photography, but I couldn't deal with it. It was too painful for me to take pictures of corpses or helicopter wrecks or children with one leg.'

Back in Sweden, Reed assisted photographer Michael Jansson before branching out on his own. Now aged forty and living in the UK, he combines advertising campaigns for a variety of brands, including fashion labels Sisley and Oui, with his own personal projects. In 2000 he held his first exhibition in Havana, an extensive portrait of the Cuban capital that incorporated his own black-and-whites with colour snapshots taken by local schoolchildren.

'I involved the children in the show because I want to get away from the element of ego in photography,' he explains. 'I found the prospect of my work filling an entire museum pretentious and nauseating. Including the kids took the seriousness out of the project and provided a different perspective on the city. I guess my approach is opposite to that of extreme narcissists like Richard Avedon and Helmut Newton. They're two of my favourites, but their presence fills the frame. In my pictures, I don't want people to think that I've been there at all.'

This deliberate detachment is evident in his *Schweppes* entry, *Amy and Jack*. Shot with a Mamiya 6x7 at a beauty spot near Reed's home in Brighton, the portrait was taken during a two-day shoot featuring young people from the area. 'I'd never met Amy or Jack before and they didn't know each other either, but it wasn't long before they starting interacting,' explains Reed, who hopes to expand the series to include other countries. 'My intention is to take the viewer back to the age of twelve or thirteen – the most honest and vital time of our lives. That's the age when we start seeing things for what they really are.'

Born to an English father and Swedish mother, Reed spent his own youth travelling back and forth between the two countries, and he believes the series is also a bid to understand his difficult childhood. 'My mother and father were just eighteen and twenty-one when I was born; they weren't ready to have a kid. For such young parents, they were drinking and partying too much and I was alone too much. I lived in a grown-up world where there weren't many kids around. I had to start taking care of myself pretty fast and, looking back, I feel I was robbed of my childhood. I lost that period of my life and now I'm trying to figure out what I missed.'

Interviewed by
Richard McClure

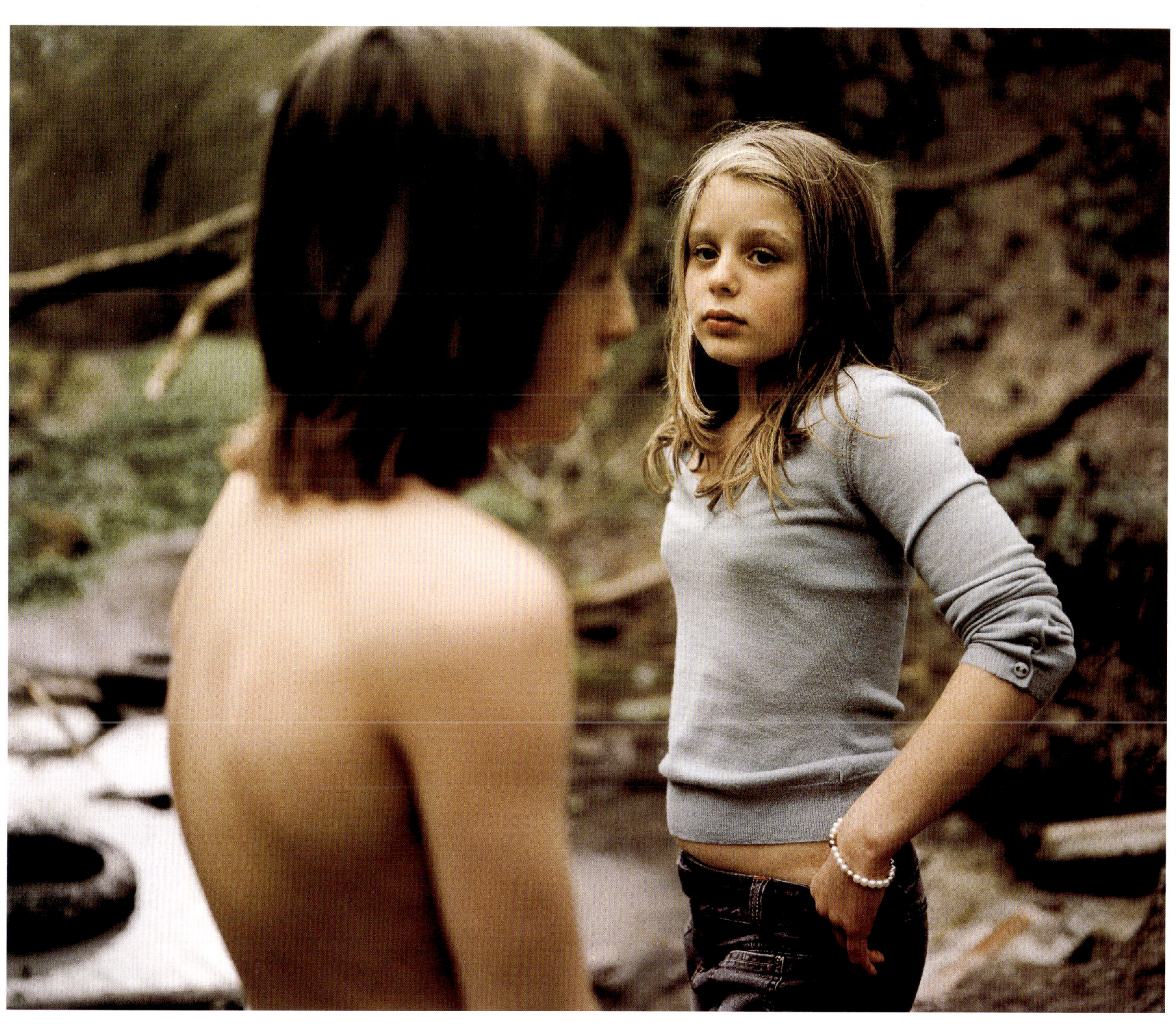

Deloitte Award Winner Karoline Hjorth

Winner of the Deloitte Award for the best portrait taken by a photographer aged twenty-five or under, Karoline Hjorth is at present studying photography at the University of Westminster in London. Aged twenty-five, she has won the prize with her first ever entry in a photographic competition. Taken from a series entitled *In Your Face*, which was exhibited in London this year as part of her degree coursework, *07.55* depicts her younger sister Siri as she wakes in the morning at Hjorth's London flat.

Wanting to examine 'notions of identity and how people represent themselves', Hjorth photographed her 18-year-old sibling at two different times of the day, with contrasting results. 'I'm interested in exploring the difference between how we look in our first moments of consciousness and how we change our appearance to represent ourselves in public later in the day,' she explains. 'The second picture in the series is a similar close-up but shows Siri with her hair done and wearing make-up and a hat. It's a very different image. Unlike *07.55*, she's very composed and fixes the viewer with a direct gaze. She's presenting herself as she wants other people to perceive her.'

Influenced by Thomas Ruff's large-scale passport-style portraits of friends and family, Hjorth initially began the project using strangers as her models but, finding the early-morning relationship 'too intimate and intrusive', she turned to photographing friends and members of her family, including her parents, grandparents and 12-year-old brother. Although Hjorth rarely uses Photoshop to manipulate her work, the portrait of Siri – taken with a medium-format Mamiya – has been slightly altered digitally to control the colours and contrast.

'The two portraits of Siri are the strongest images in the series mainly because of our close relationship, but also because of her age,' says Hjorth. 'There's a lot of pressure on young women to present the perfect image, and Siri is still trying to figure out who she is. She's struggling with life a bit and her vulnerability comes across. It's also quite an ambiguous image, which I like. Her face often looks very red in the morning because of a skin condition, but to some people it looks like she's been crying.'

Born in Trondheim, Norway, Hjorth studied anthropology at the University of Oslo before deciding that her heart lay in photography. Enrolling at Cleveland College of Art and Design in 2003, she soon tired of Middlesbrough's 'post-industrial grime' and transferred to the University of Westminster. After completing her degree, she hopes to remain in London and work as a freelance photographer. 'I'm fascinated by different cultures and societies, but in anthropology I was forced to be very objective,' she says. 'Photography allows me to be more subjective and gives me much more freedom. I love meeting people and connecting with them. Now I can use my camera to understand what makes people tick.'

Interviewed by Richard McClure

Karoline Hjorth 07.55
from the series
In Your Face
March 2005

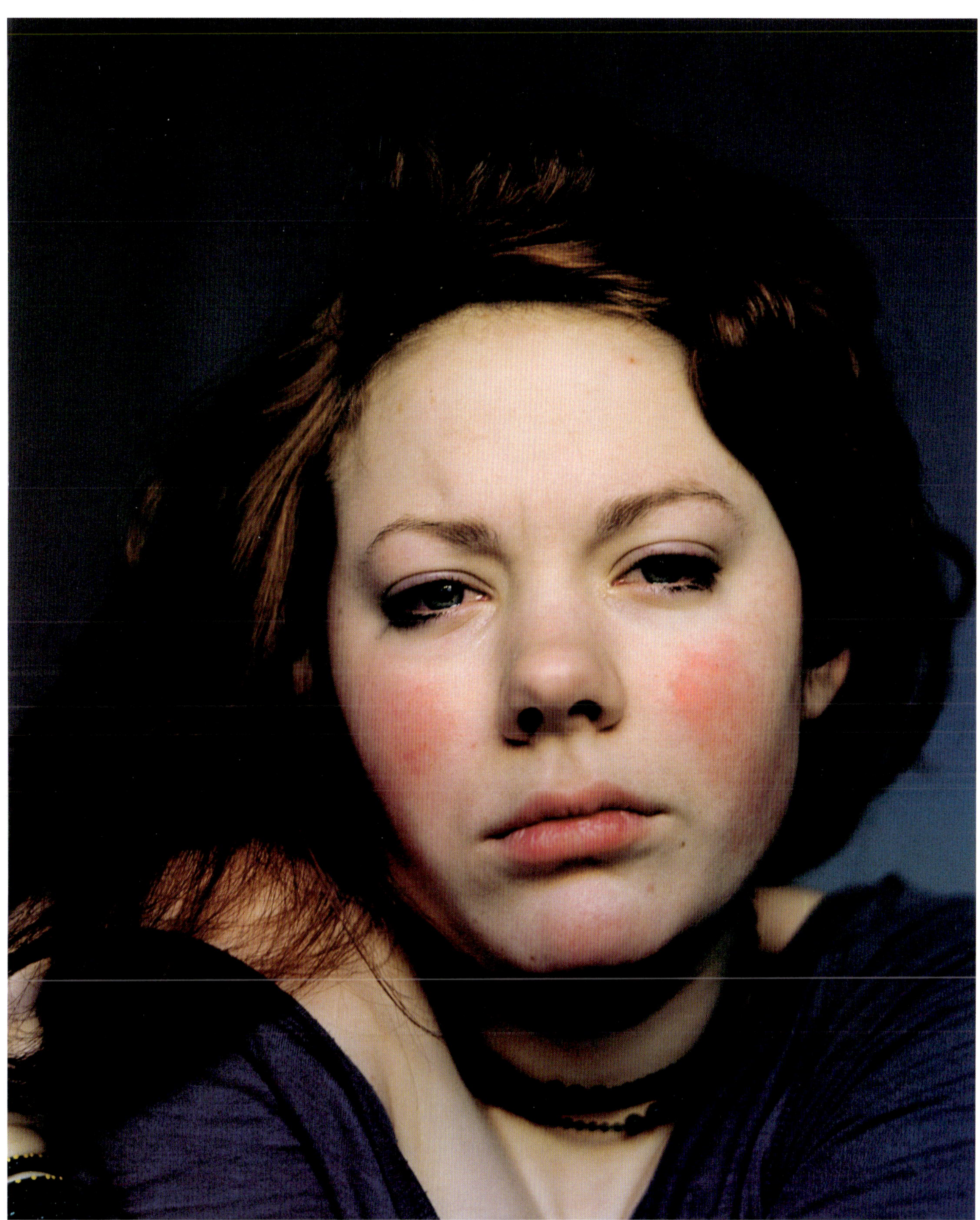

Exhibitors

Anna
February 2005

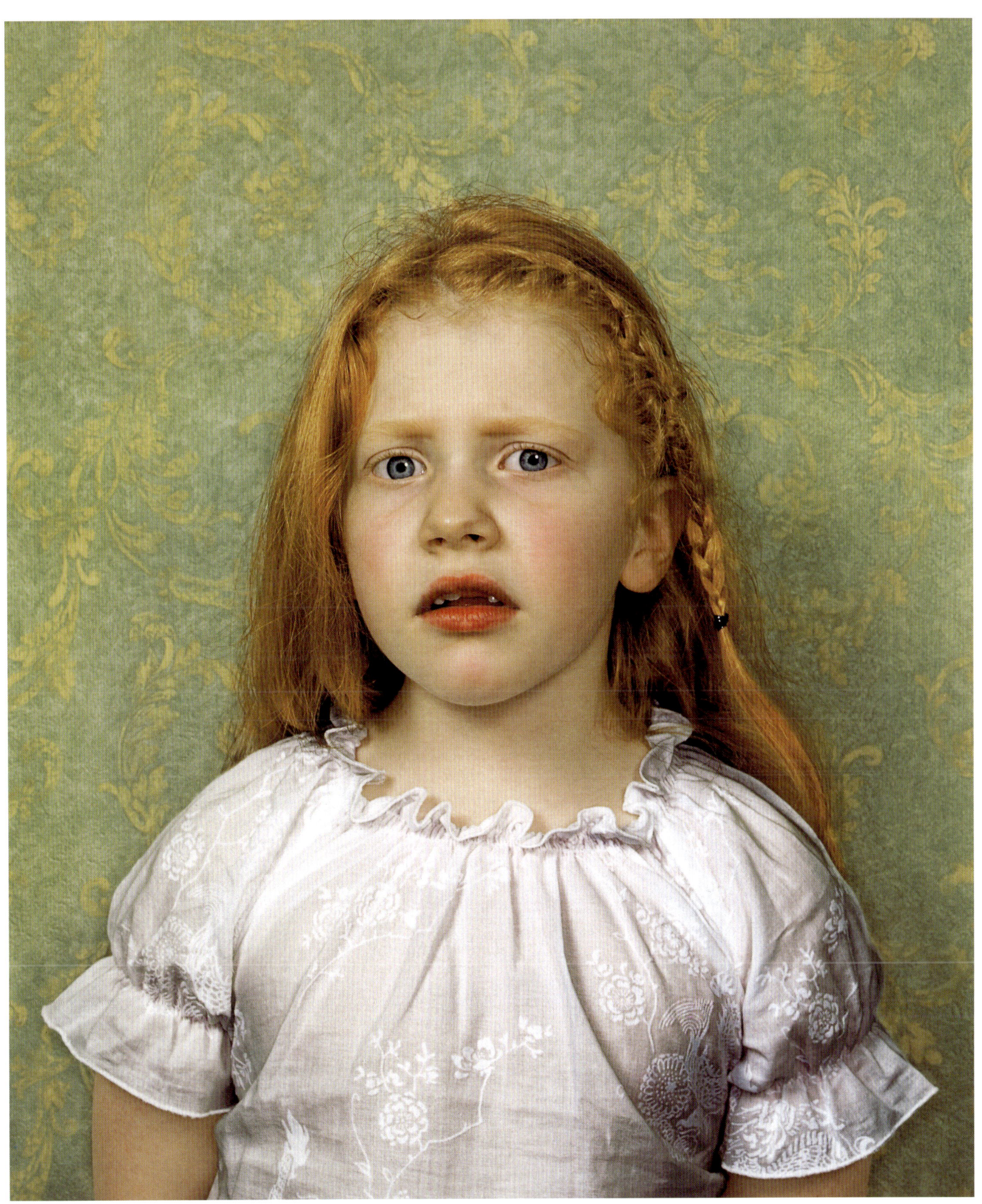

Shane Deegan Rebecca
May 2005

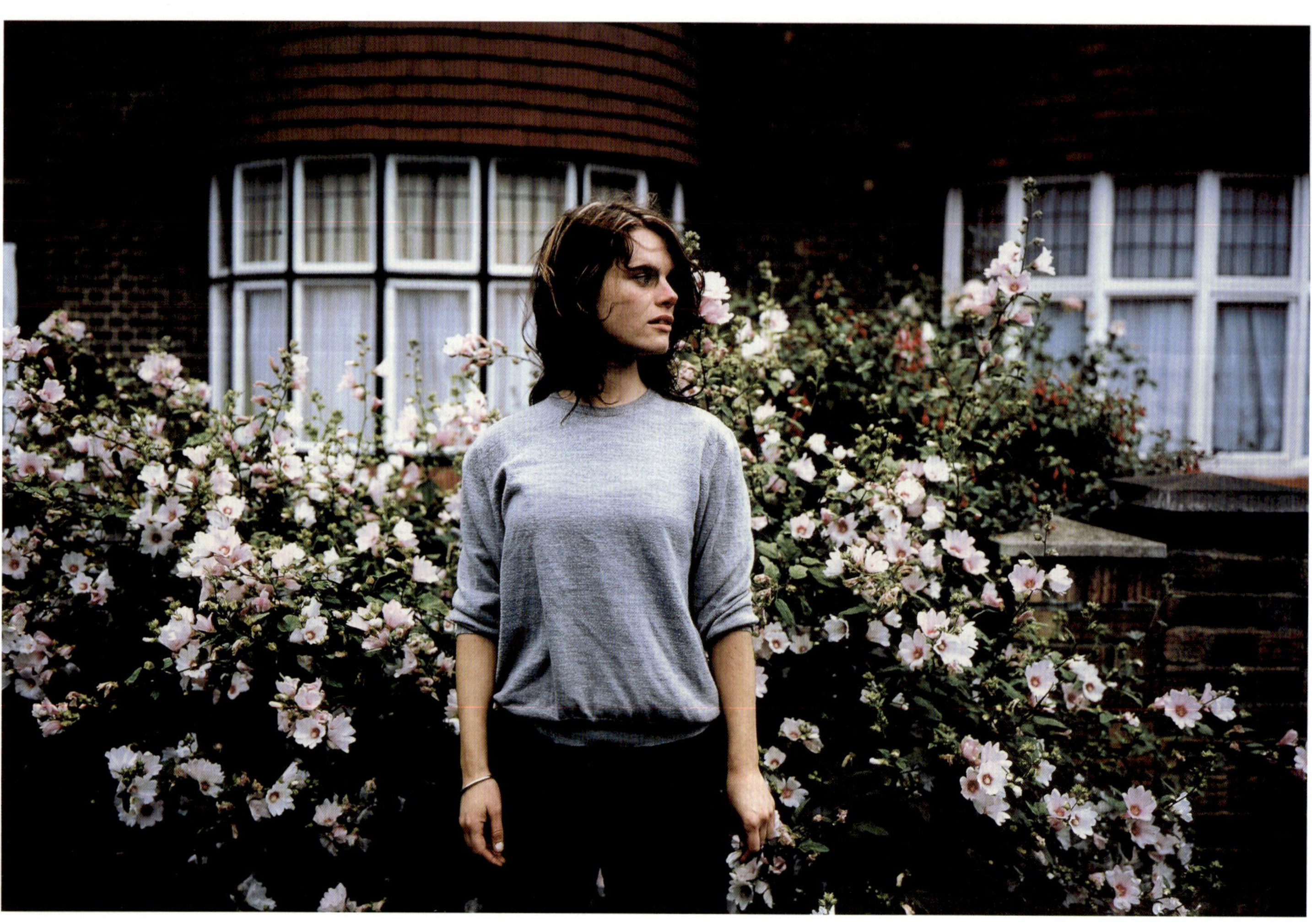

Clarissa Leahy

Lucy and Her Tent
March 2005

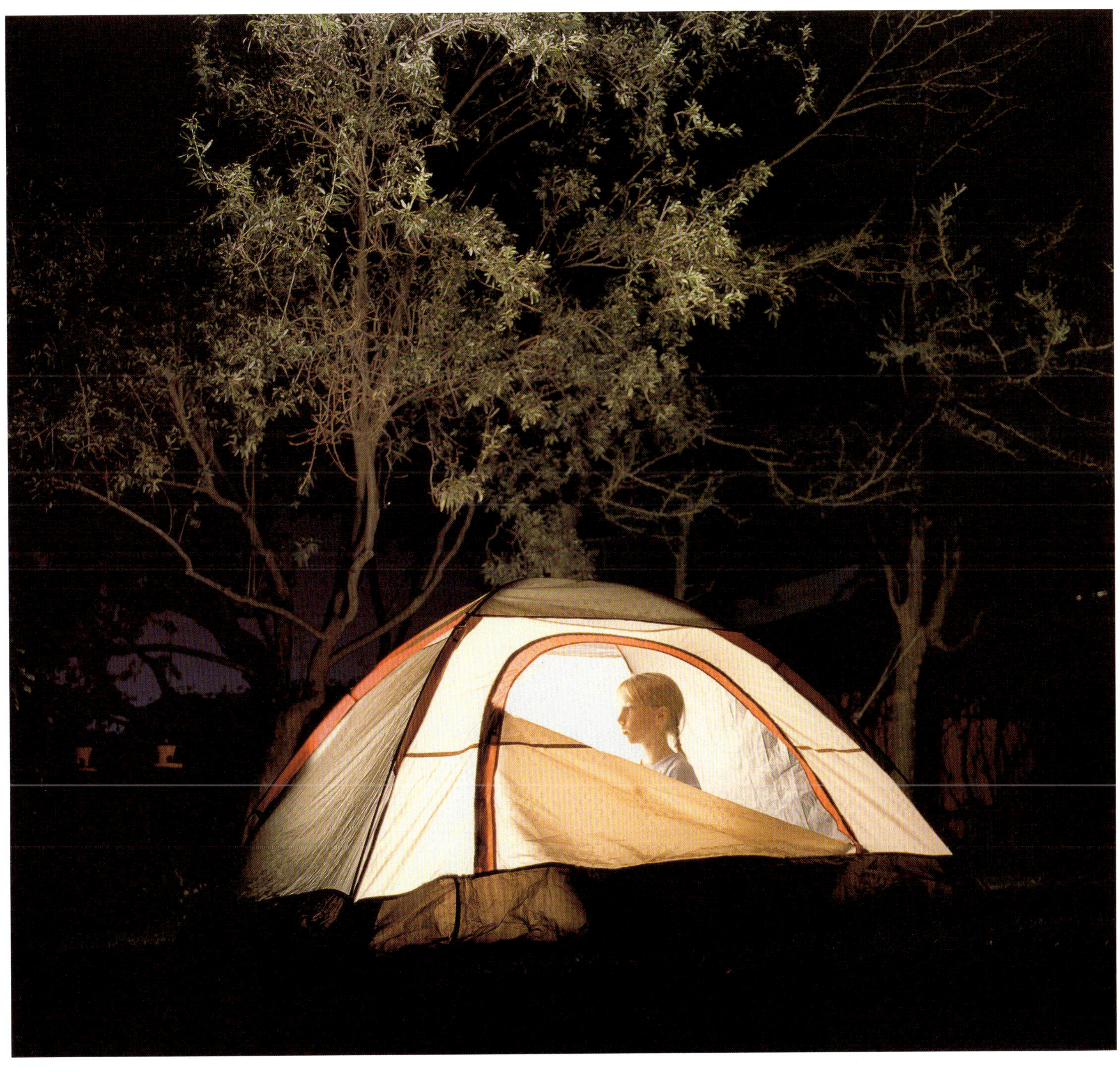

Daniel Slimm

Rosie *from the series* Durley, Hampshire
May 2005

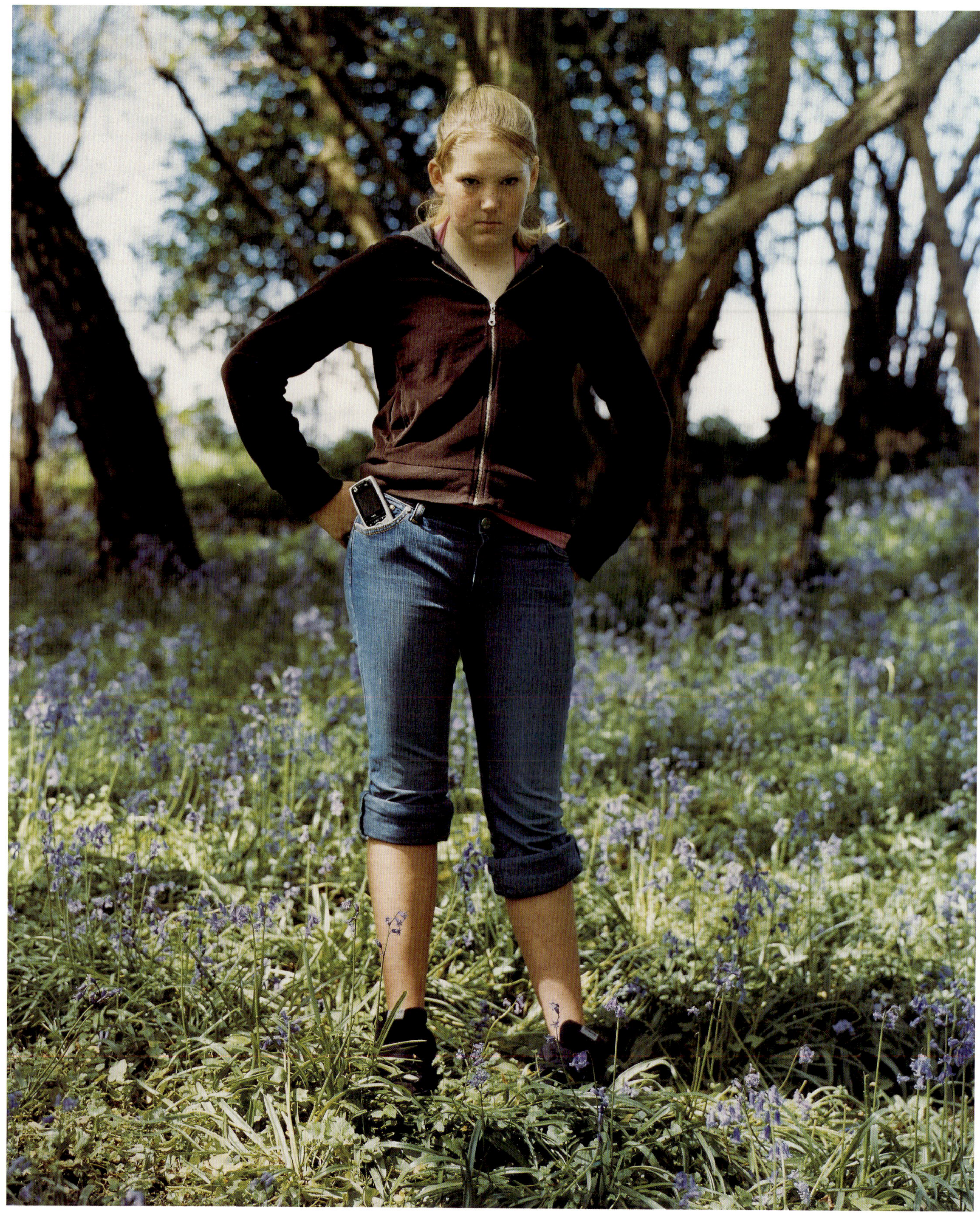

Paul Blake

Tony Saddique,
Red Star Harehills,
Leeds *from the series*
Sport for Sport's Sake
December 2004

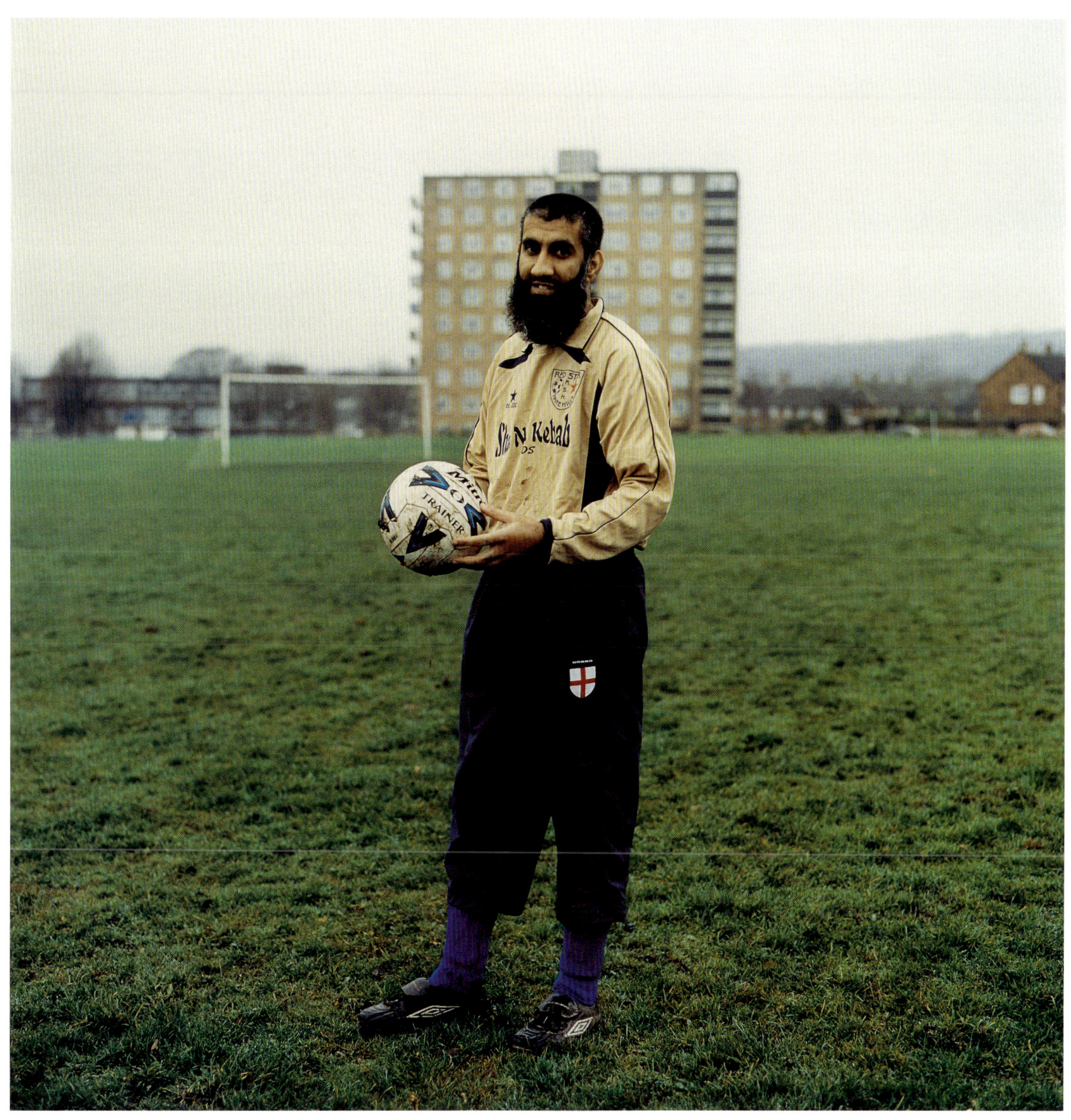

Maro Ambrosi

Portraits in Black 02
from the series
Portraits in Black
February 2004

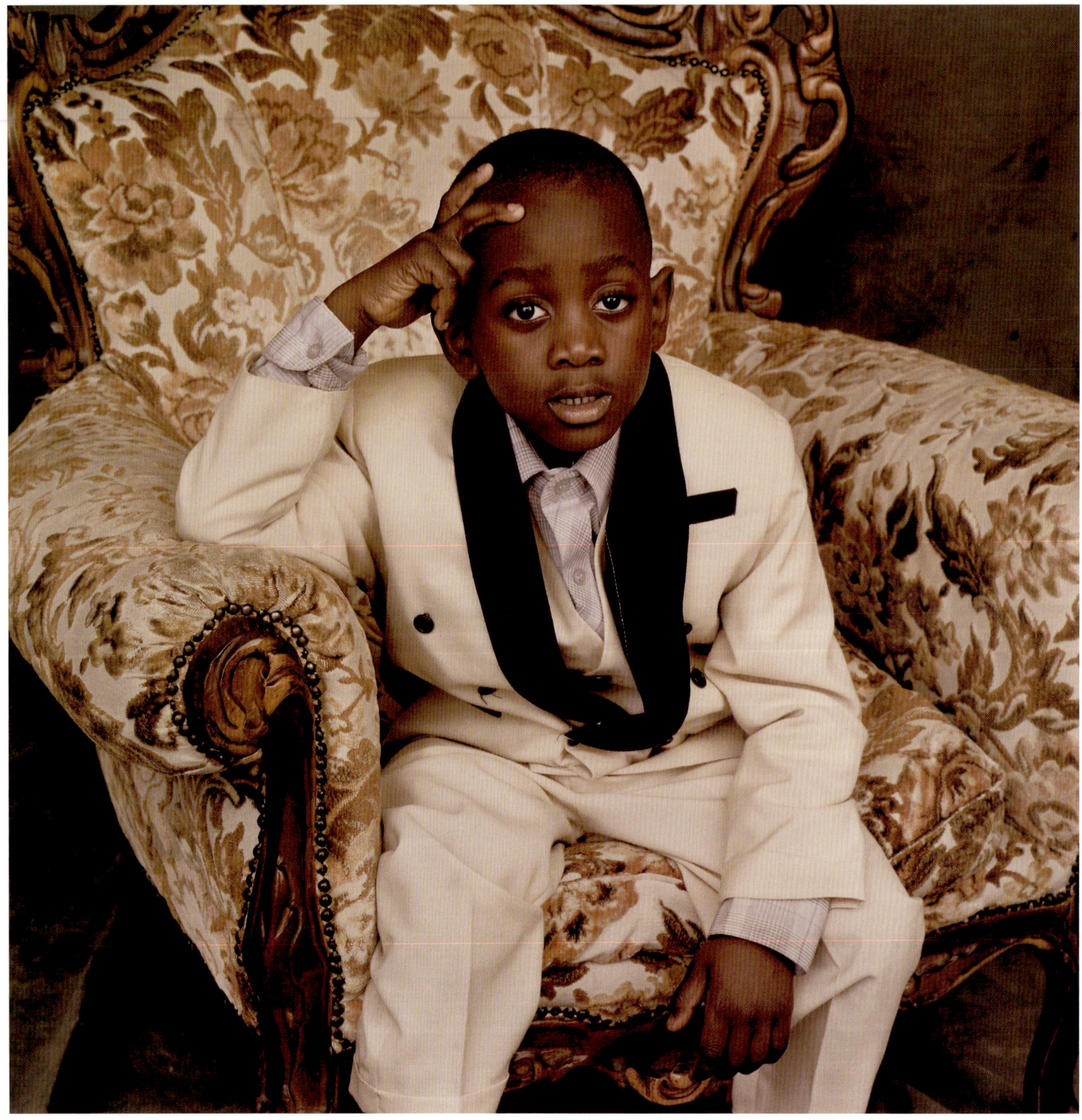

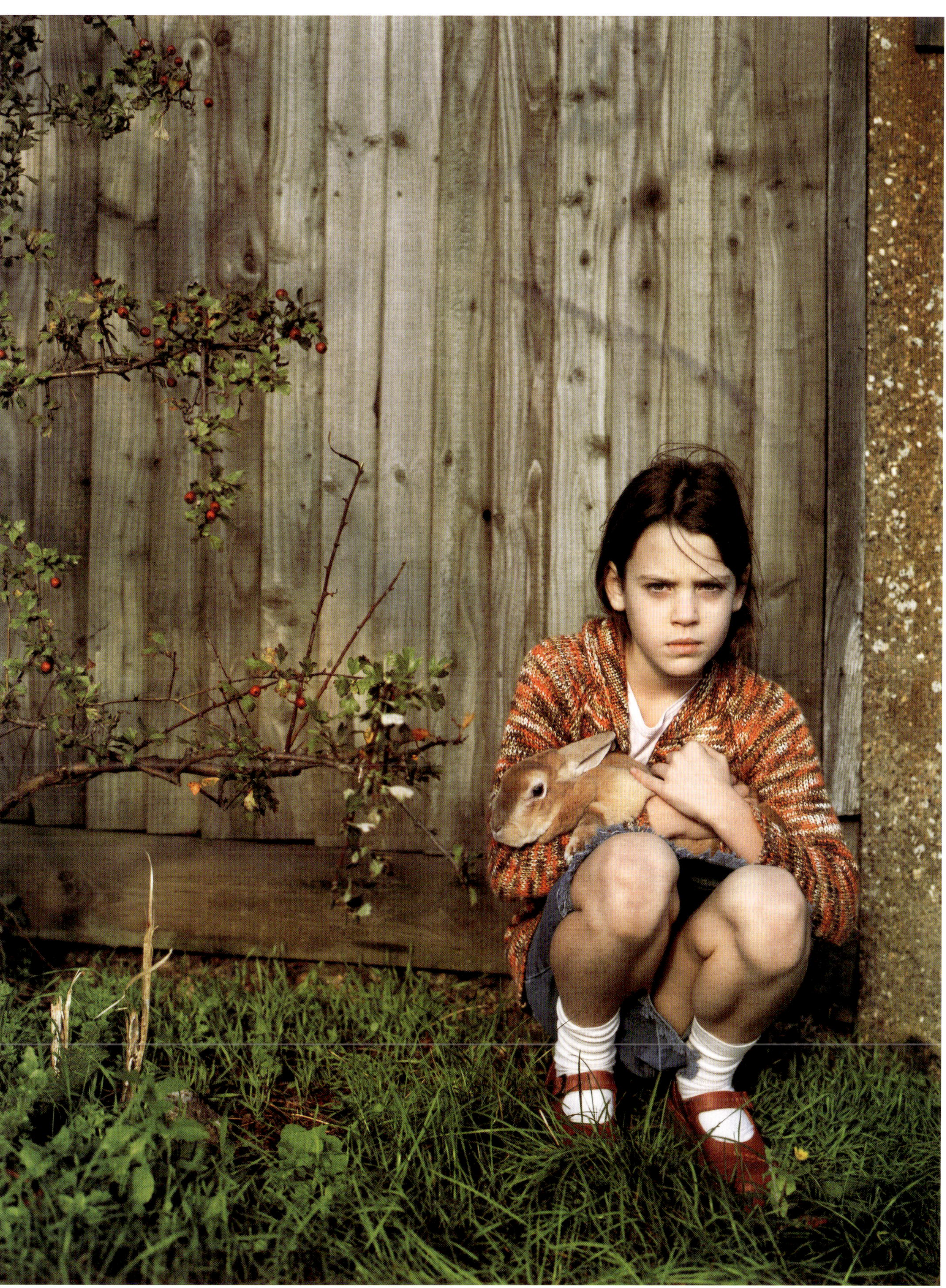

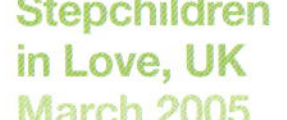
Richard Ansett

Stepchildren
in Love, UK
March 2005

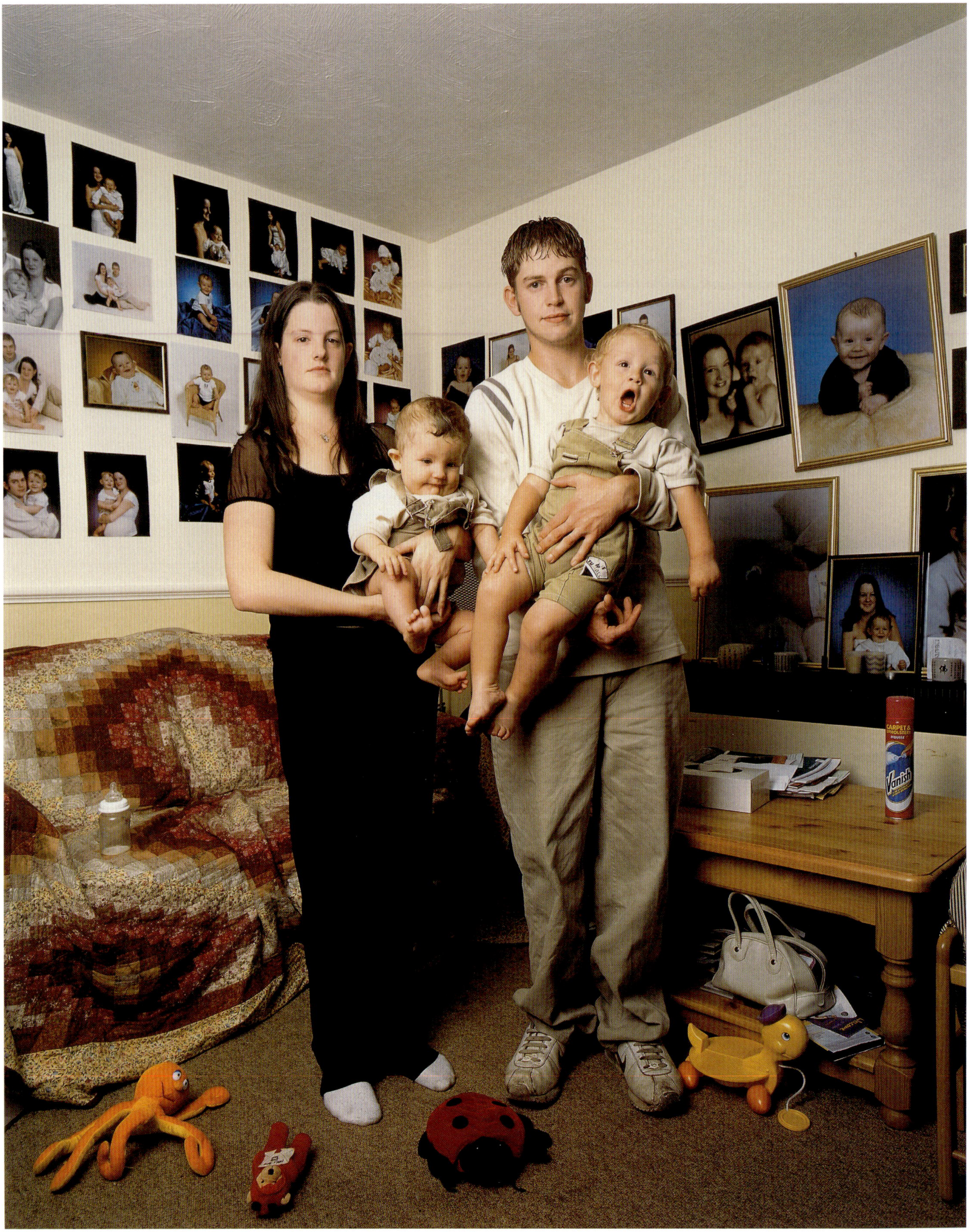

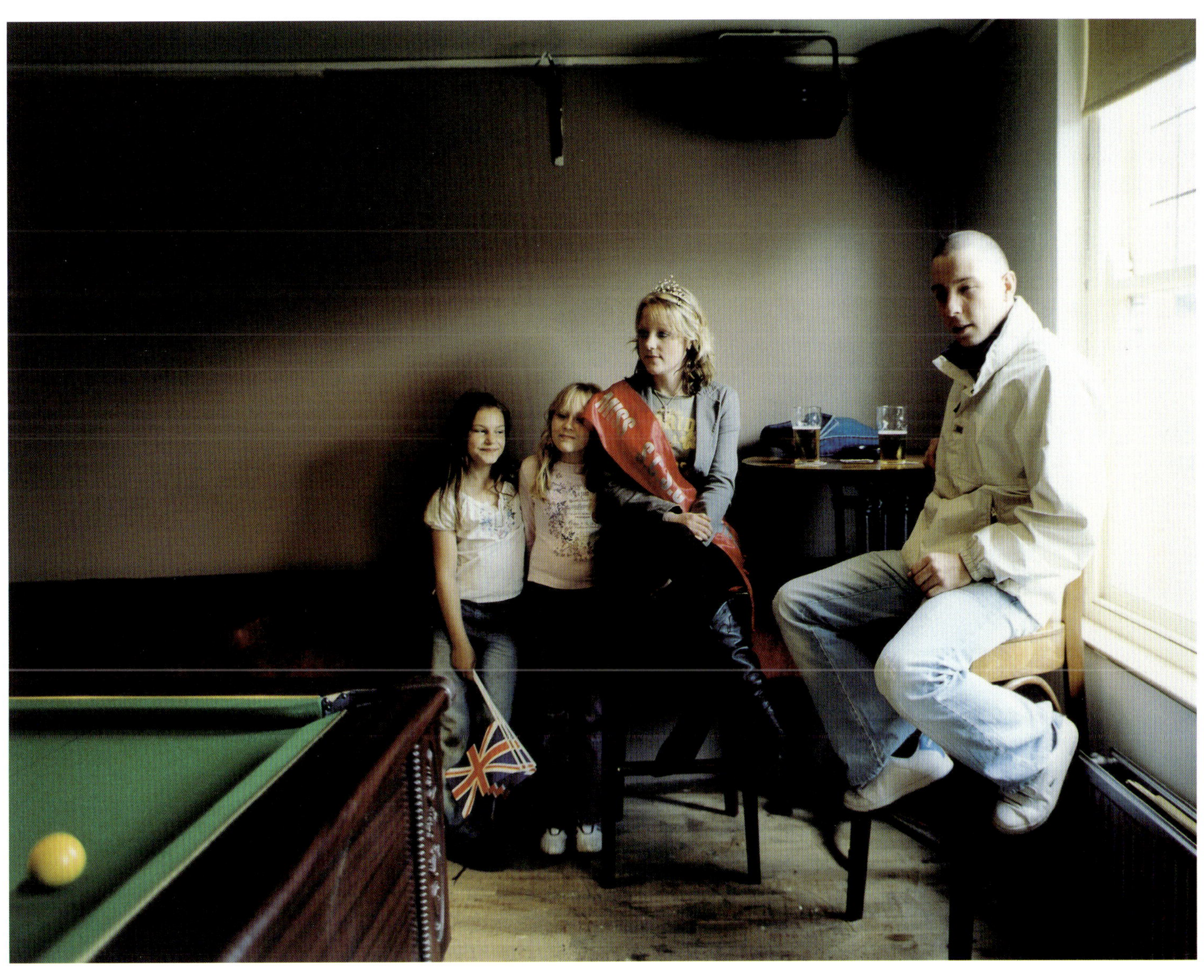

David Scheinmann

Ballet Girls
April 2005

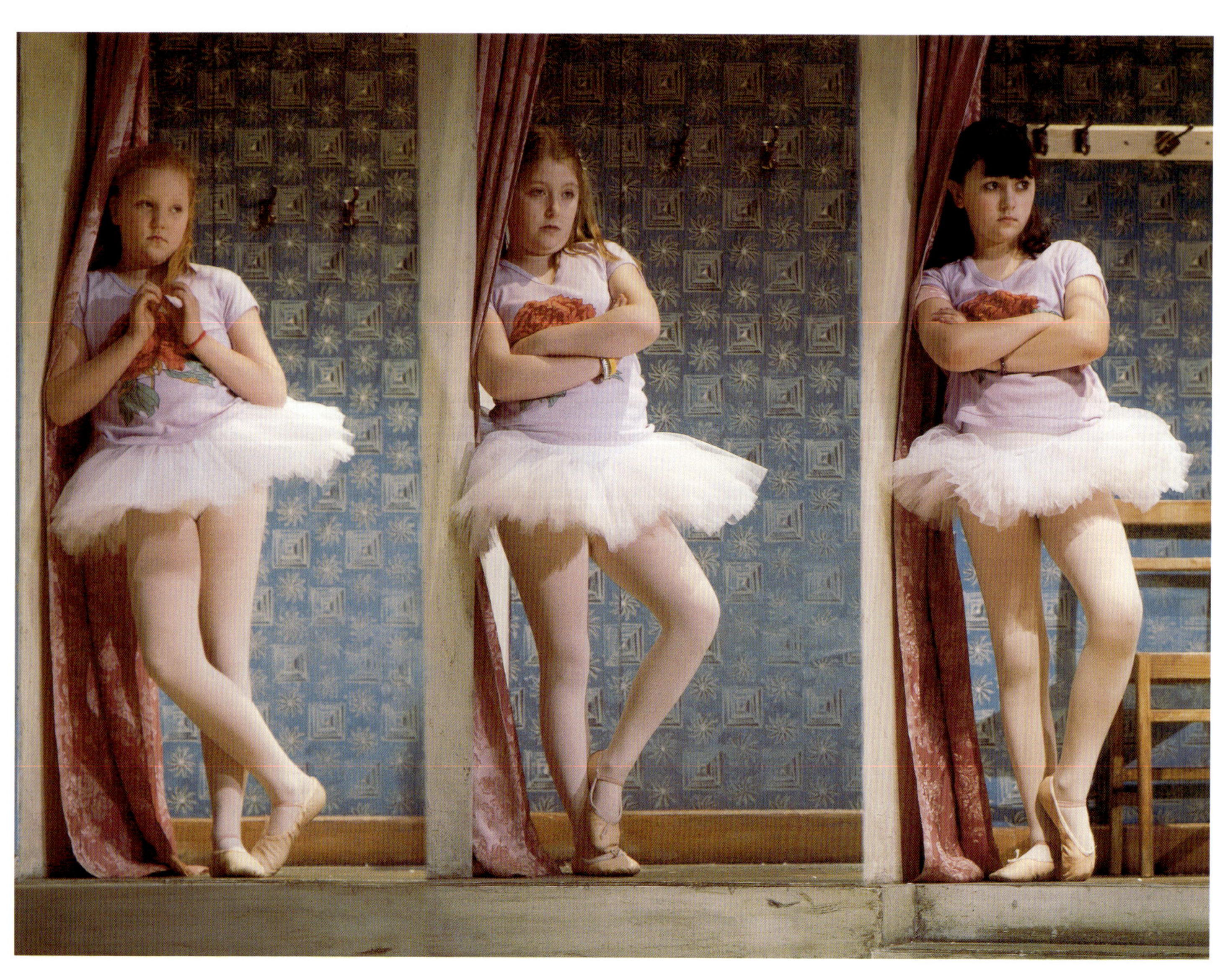

Elizabeth Zeschin

Hebe in Pool
May 2005

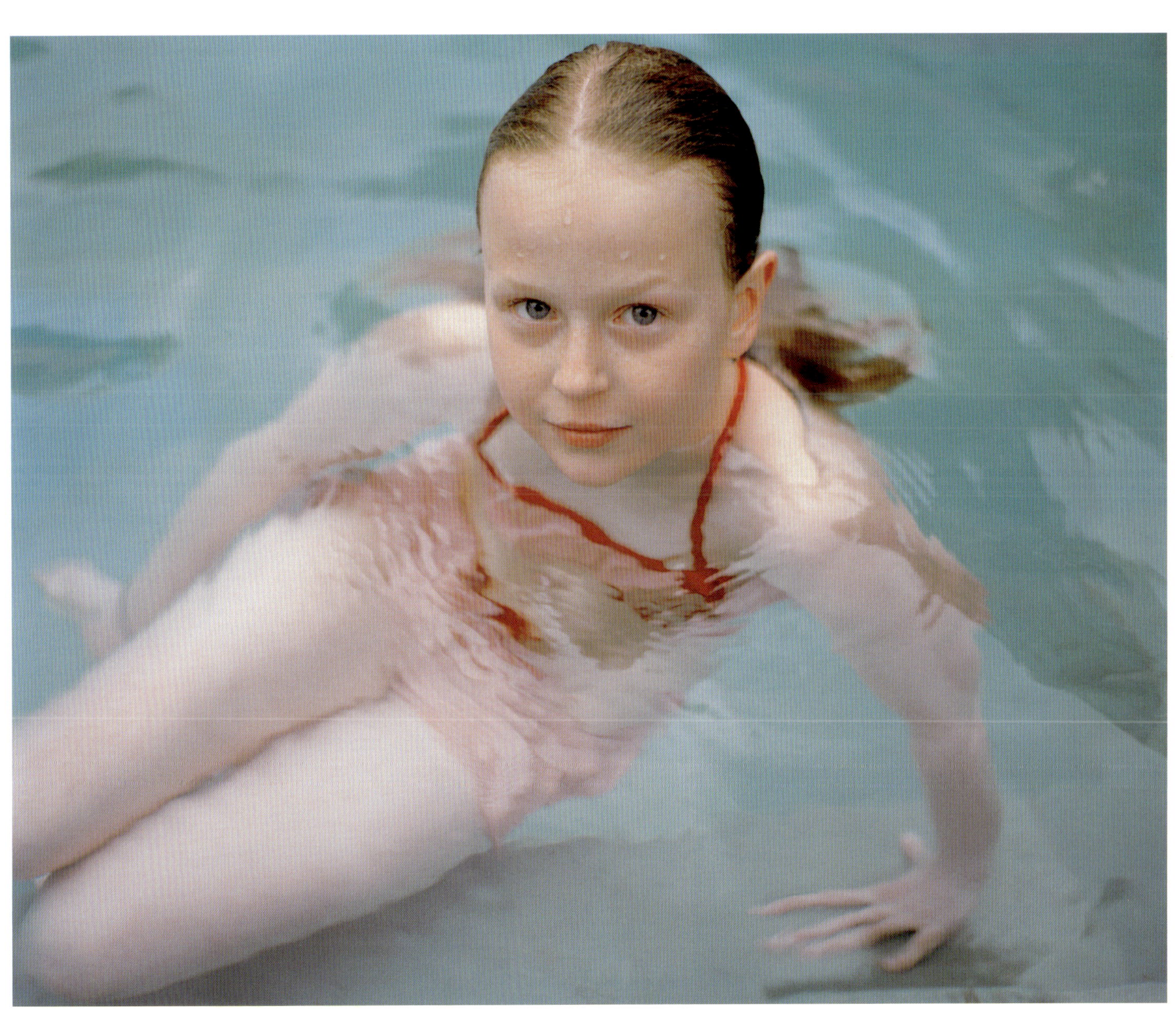

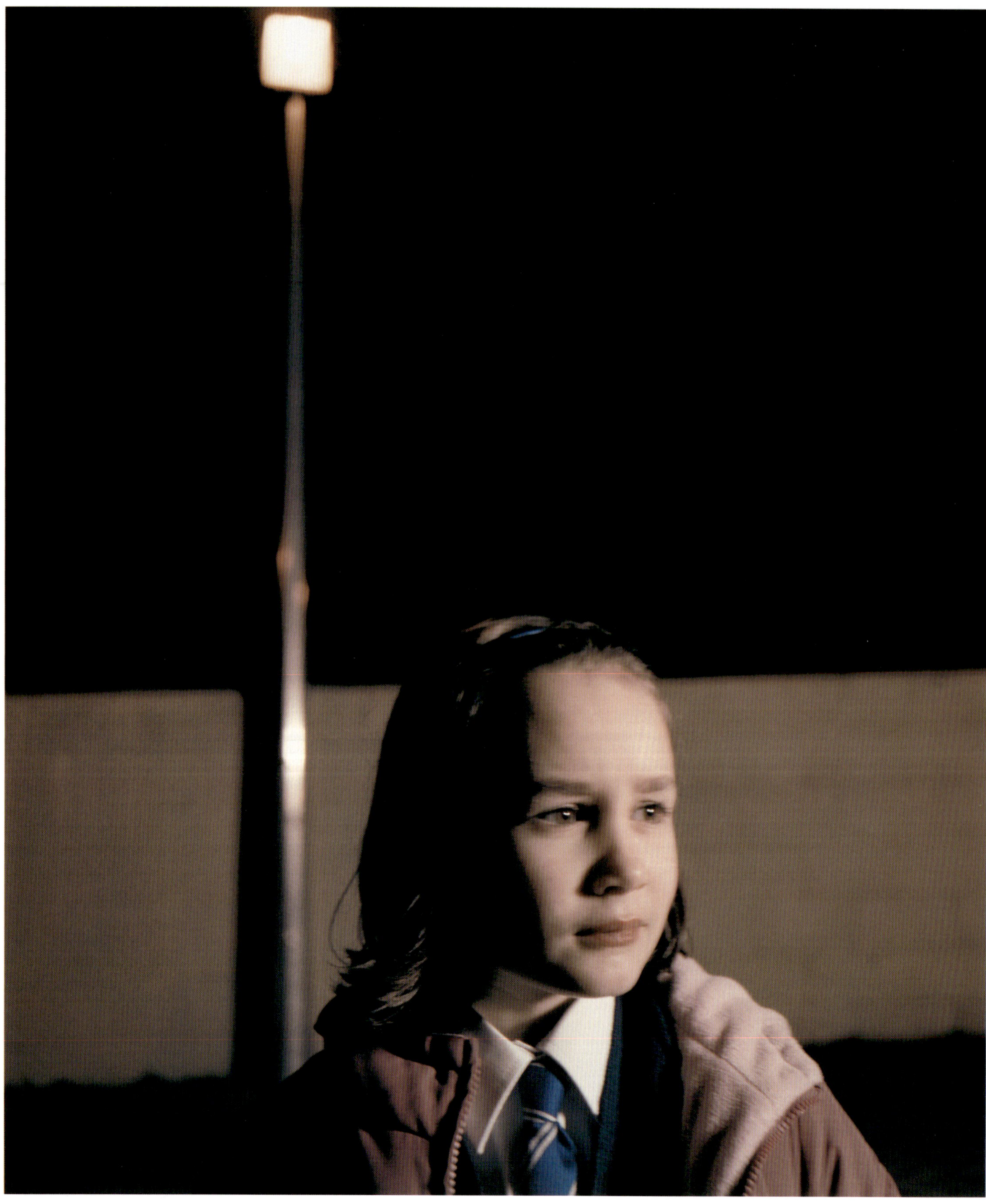

Anton Want

Chlóe – Racecourse Park *from the series* Cyclists
January 2005

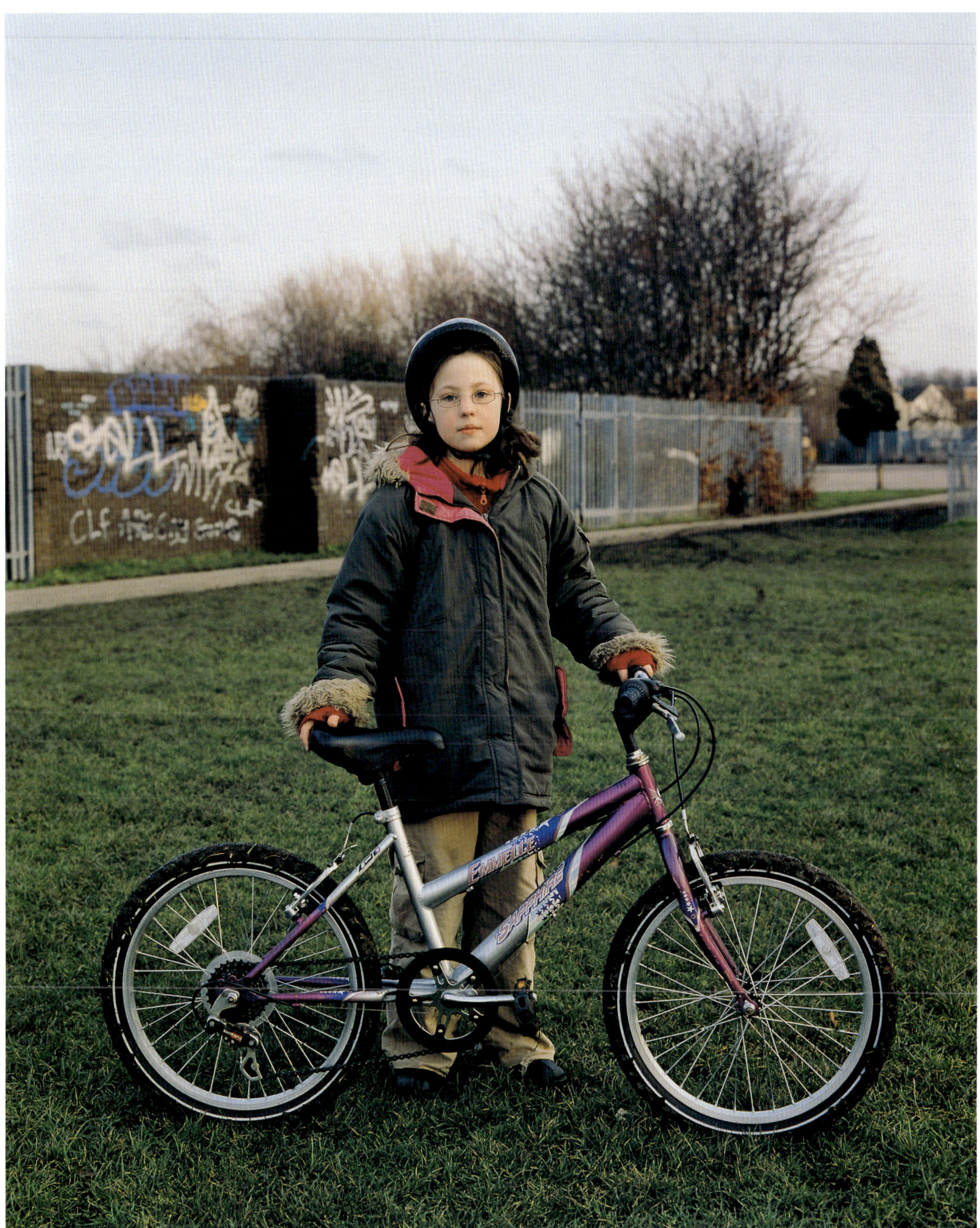

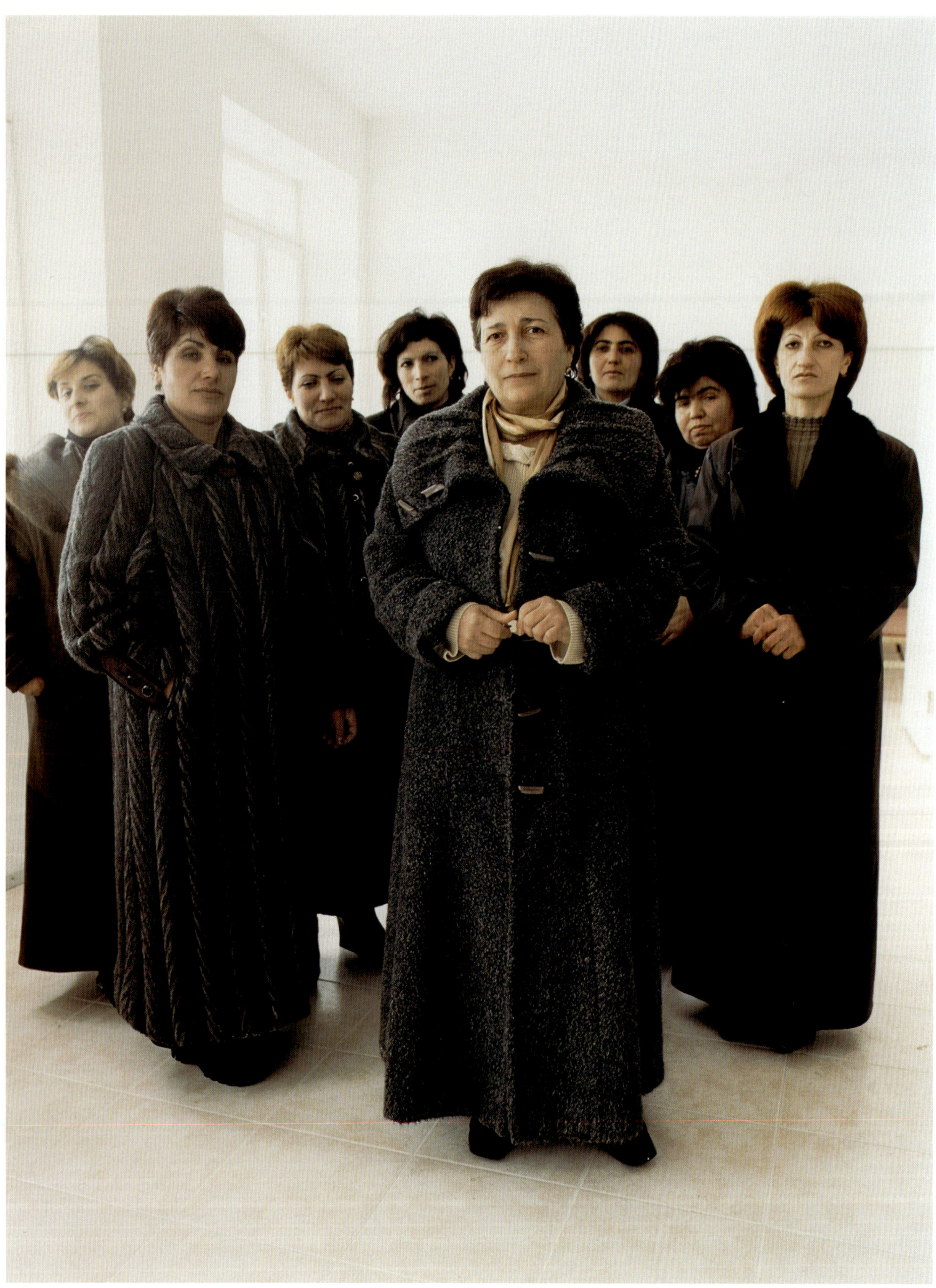

Michal Chelbin

Sasha
September 2004

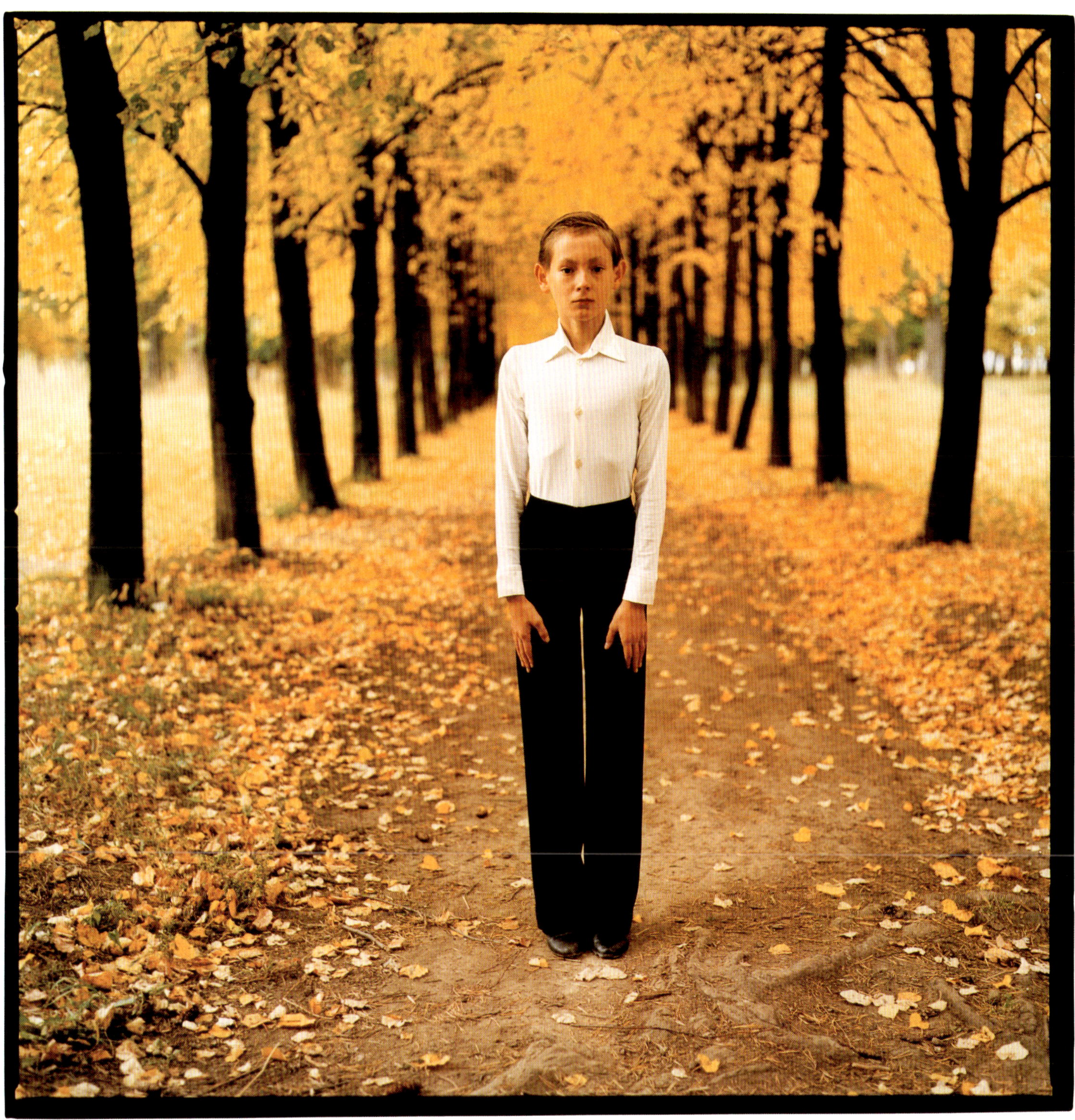

Matthew Hawkins

Vetch Girls
May 2005

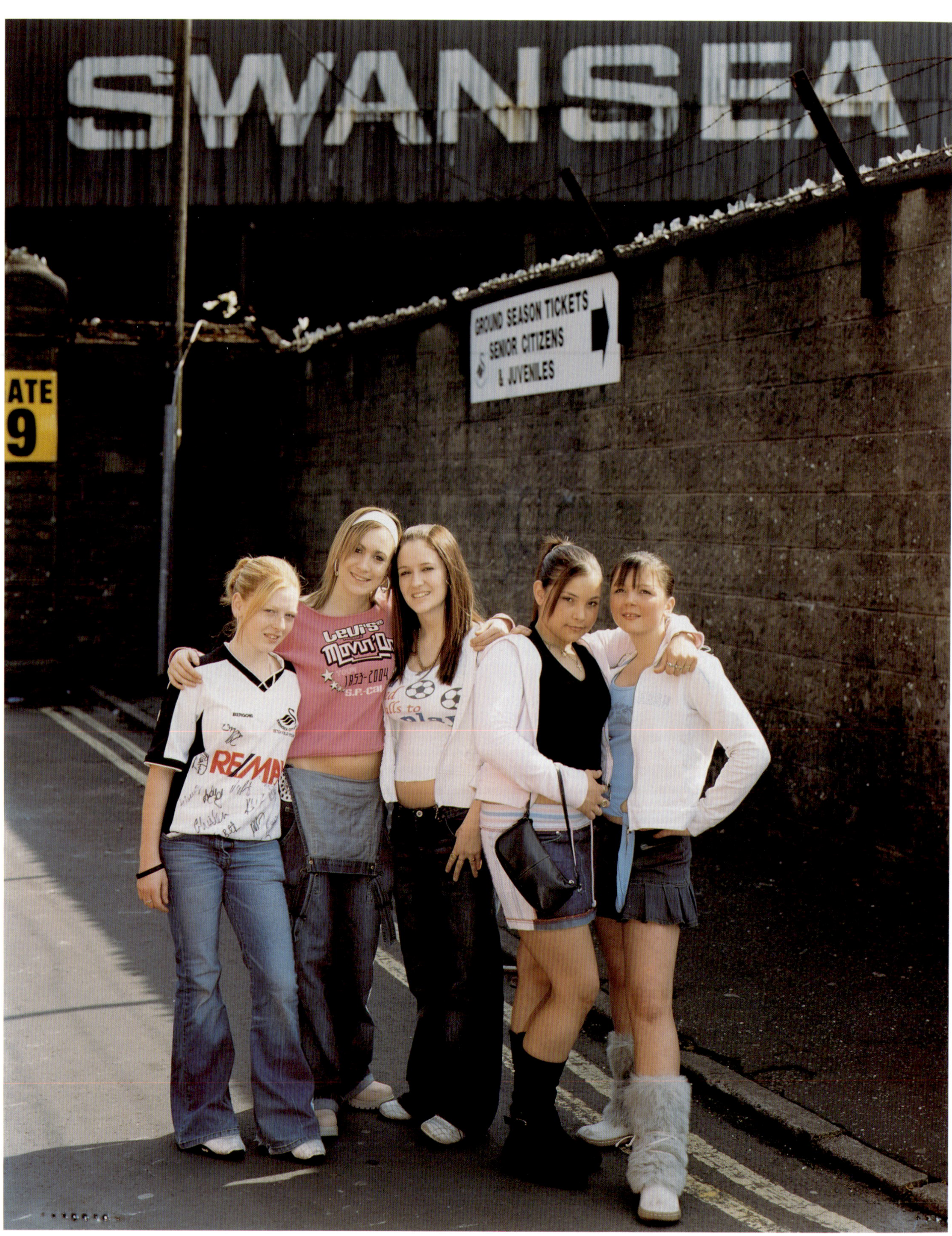

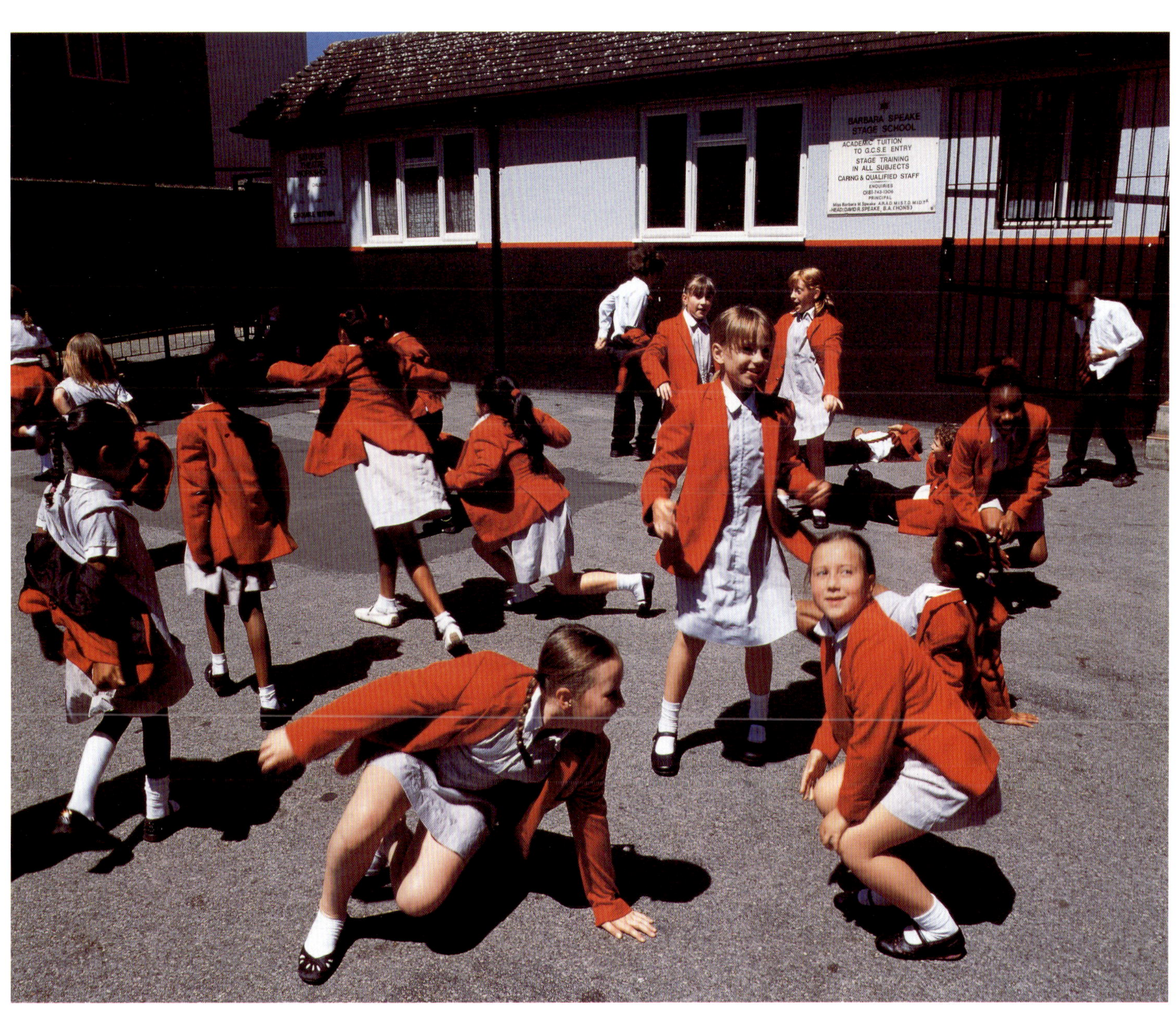
BARBARA SPEAKE
STAGE SCHOOL
ACADEMIC TUITION
TO G.C.S.E ENTRY
STAGE TRAINING
IN ALL SUBJECTS
CARING & QUALIFIED STAFF
ENQUIRIES
0181-743-1306
PRINCIPAL
HEAD: DAVID R. SPEAKE B.A. (HONS)

Gillian Laub

Samar and Rauan
from the series
Common Ground –
Portraits and
Testimonials
of Israelis and
Palestinians
June 2004

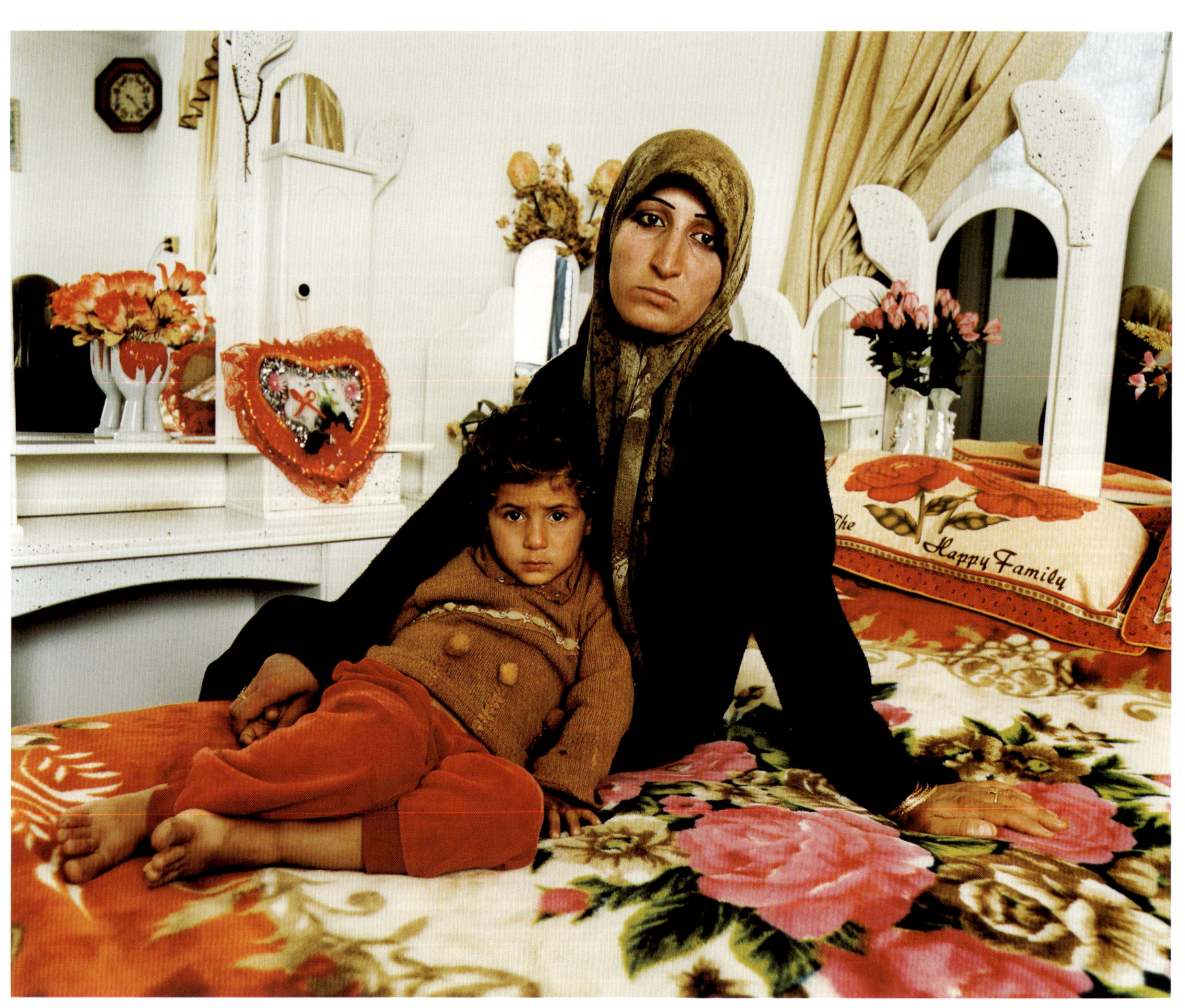

Tara Darby

Delaine in Her Room
from the series Room
April 2005

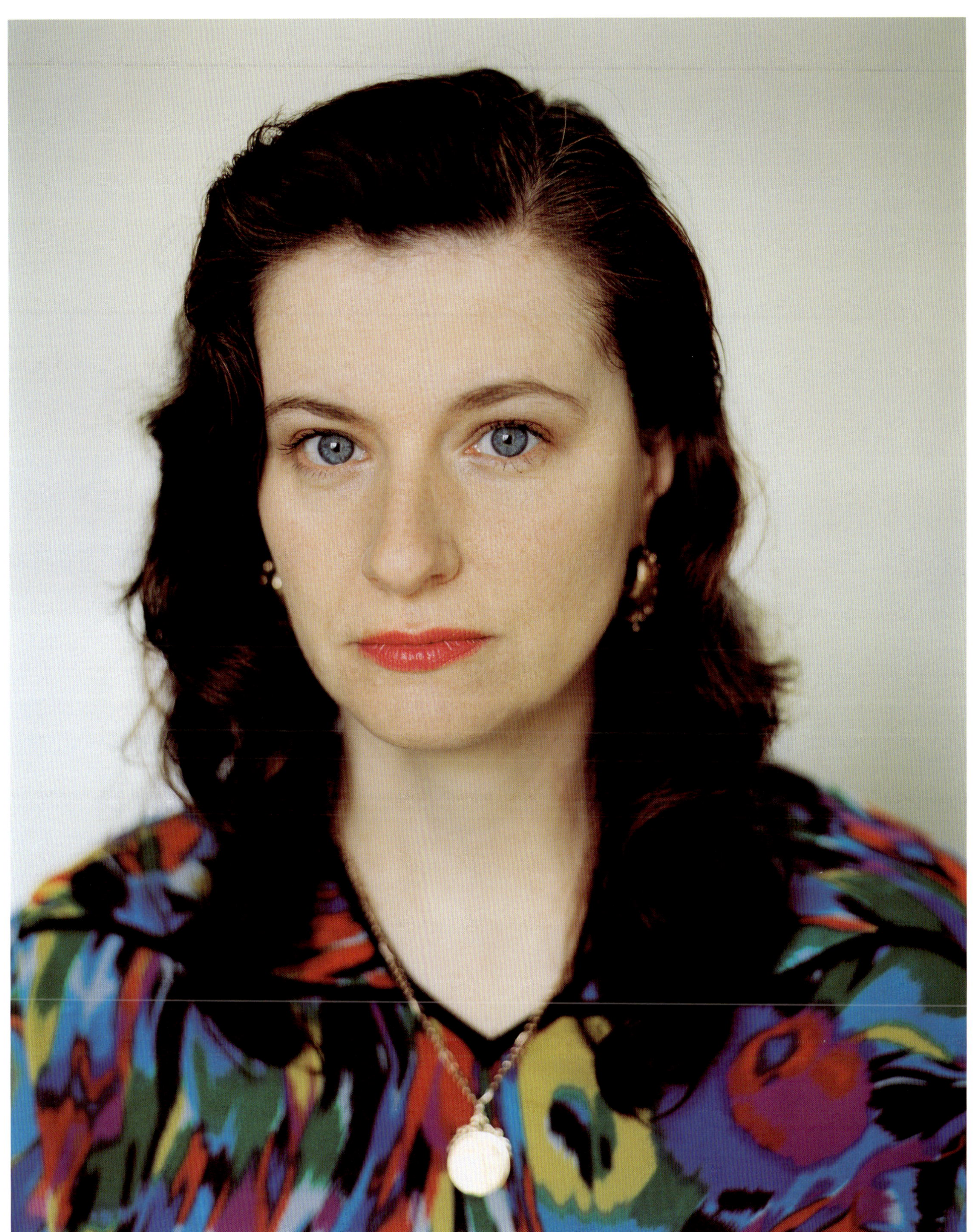

Naomi Harris

Miss Lifestyles, Her Husband and Friends *from the series* White Picket Fences – Swinging in the Suburbs July 2004

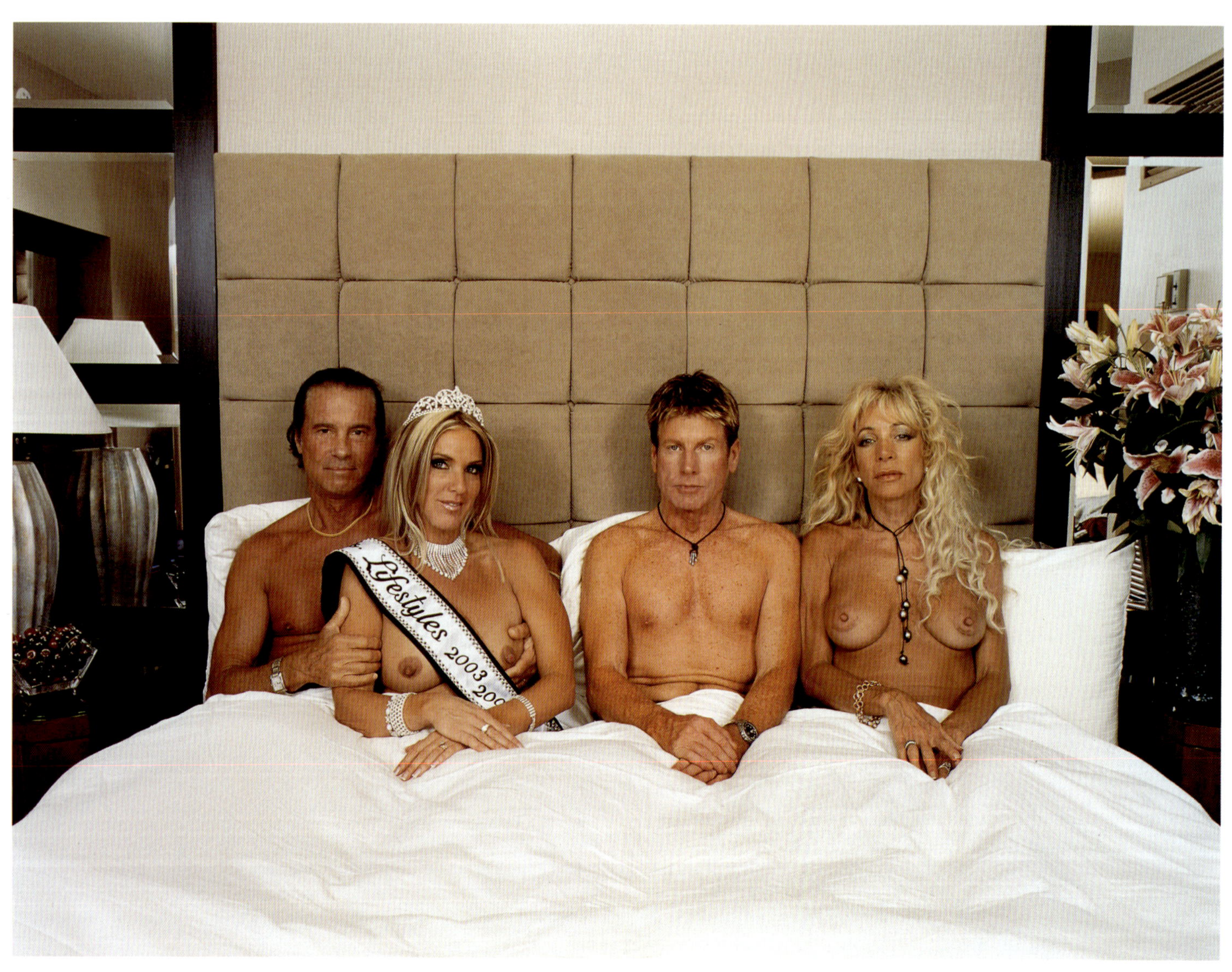

Sheila Barry

Bryan
from the series
Being Sixteen
April 2005

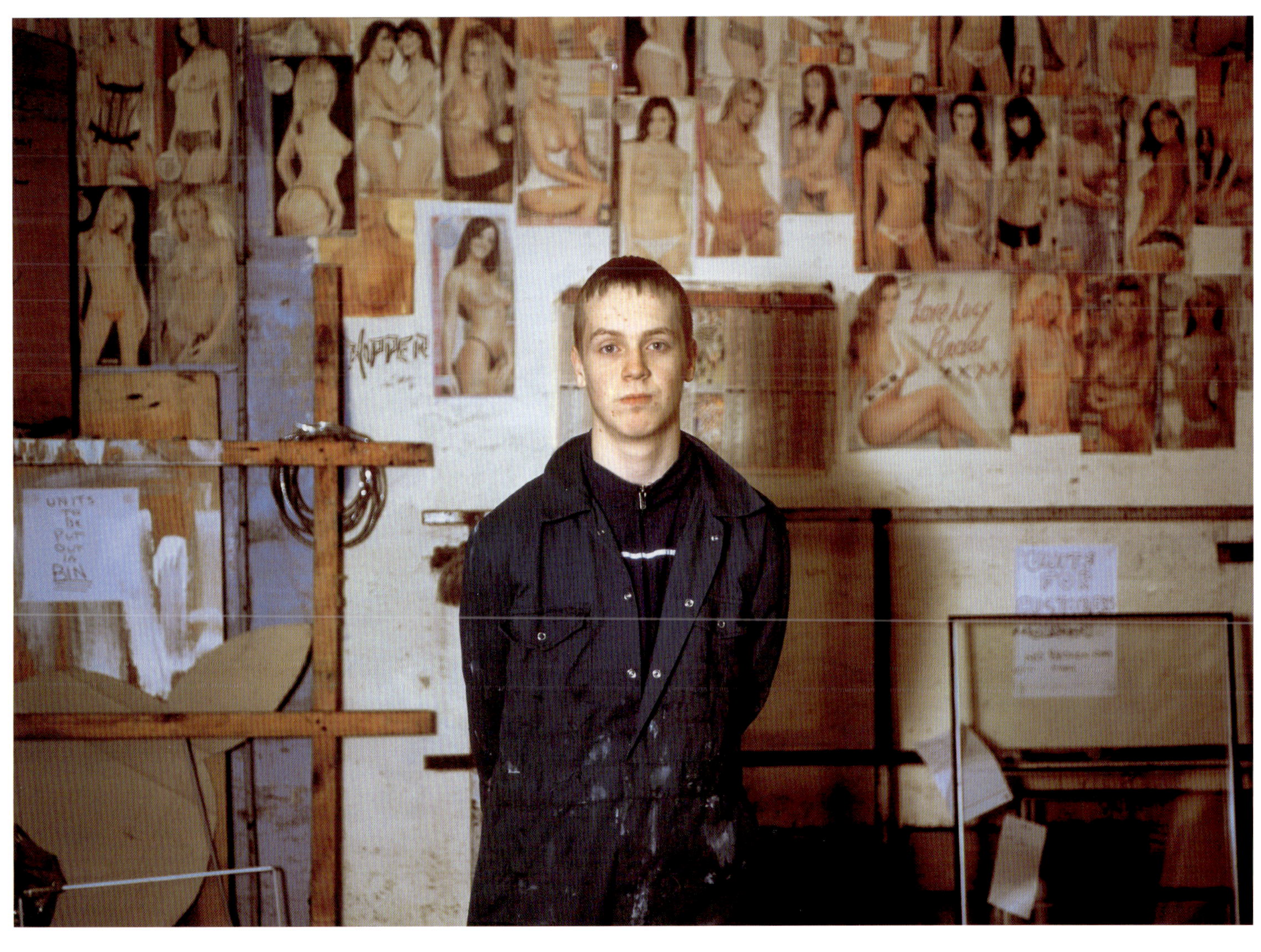

Pål Christopher Hansen

Dax & Susie – Teenage Parents
from the series
Teenage Parents UK
September 2004

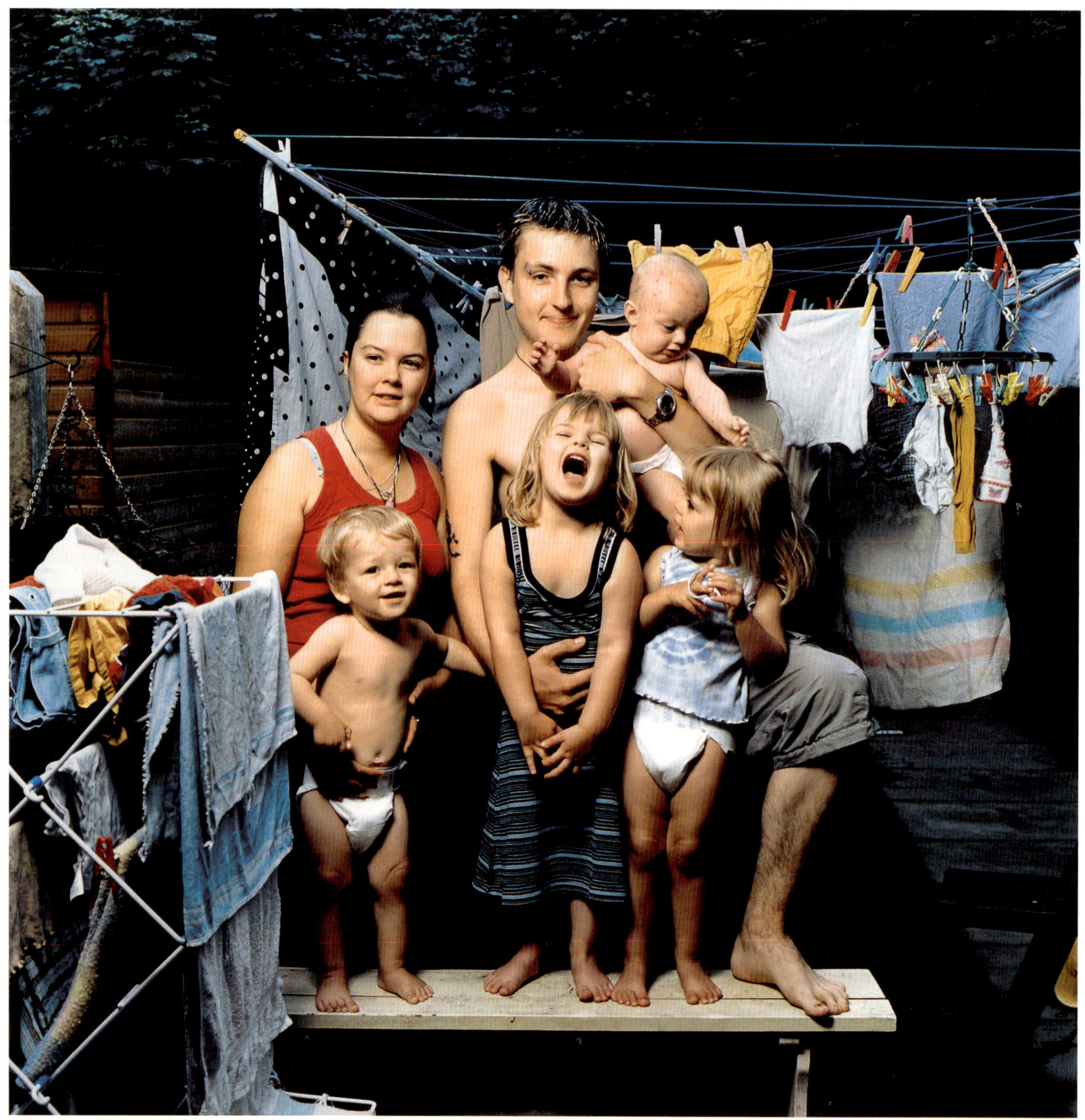

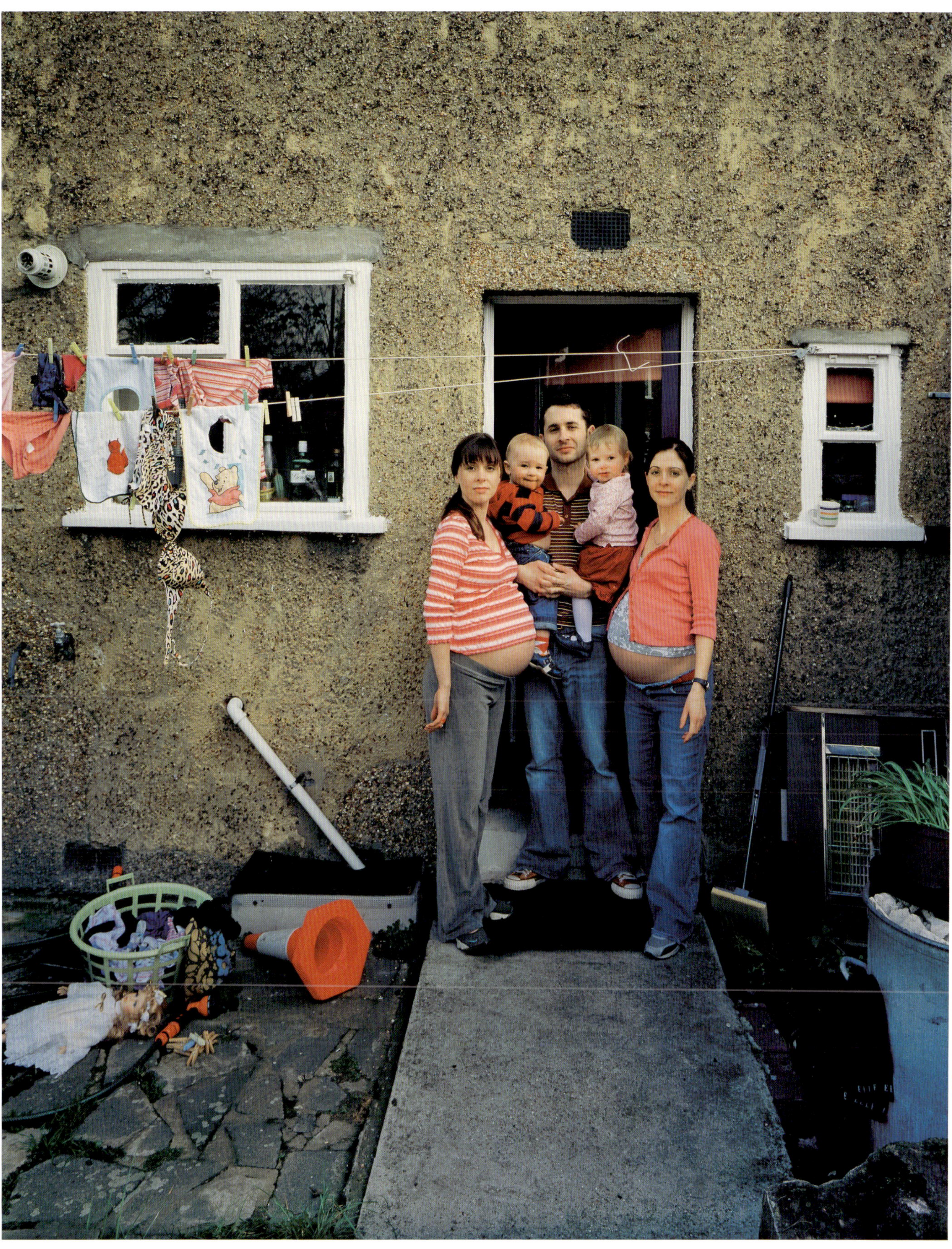

Nadav Kander

Cowboy,
Los Angeles
January 2005

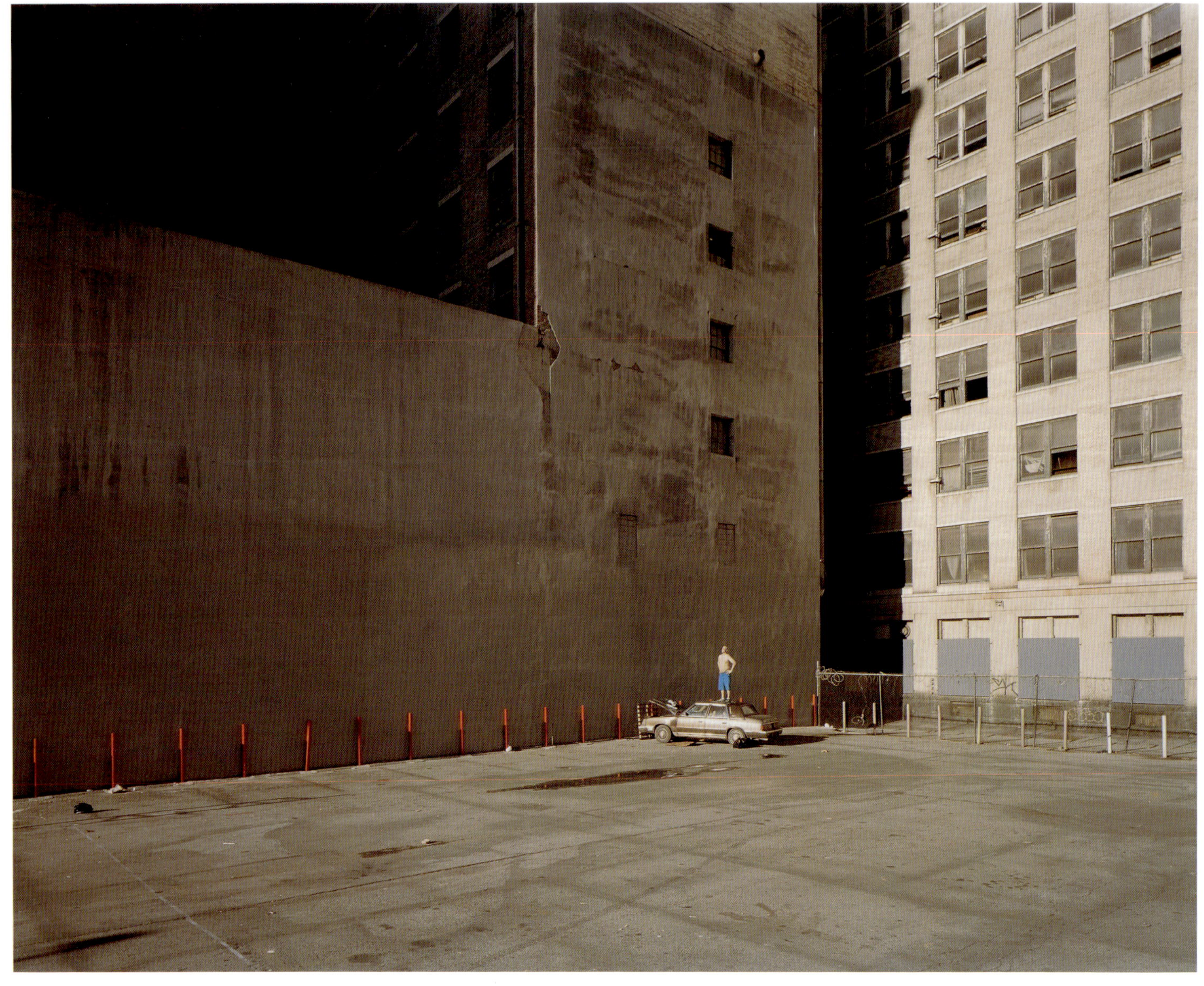

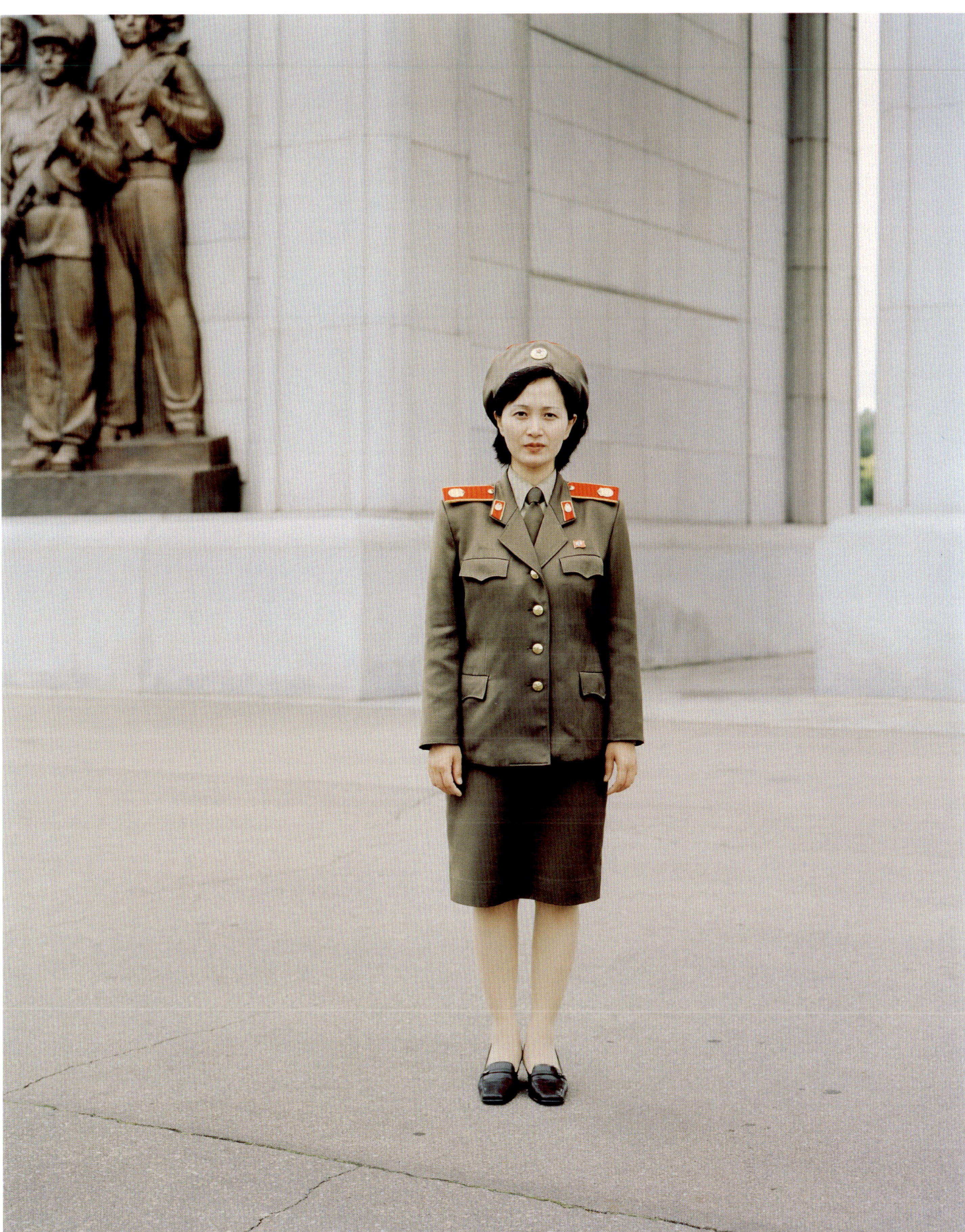

Christopher Lane

St John Ambulance, Northampton
from the series
Thinking of England
November 2004

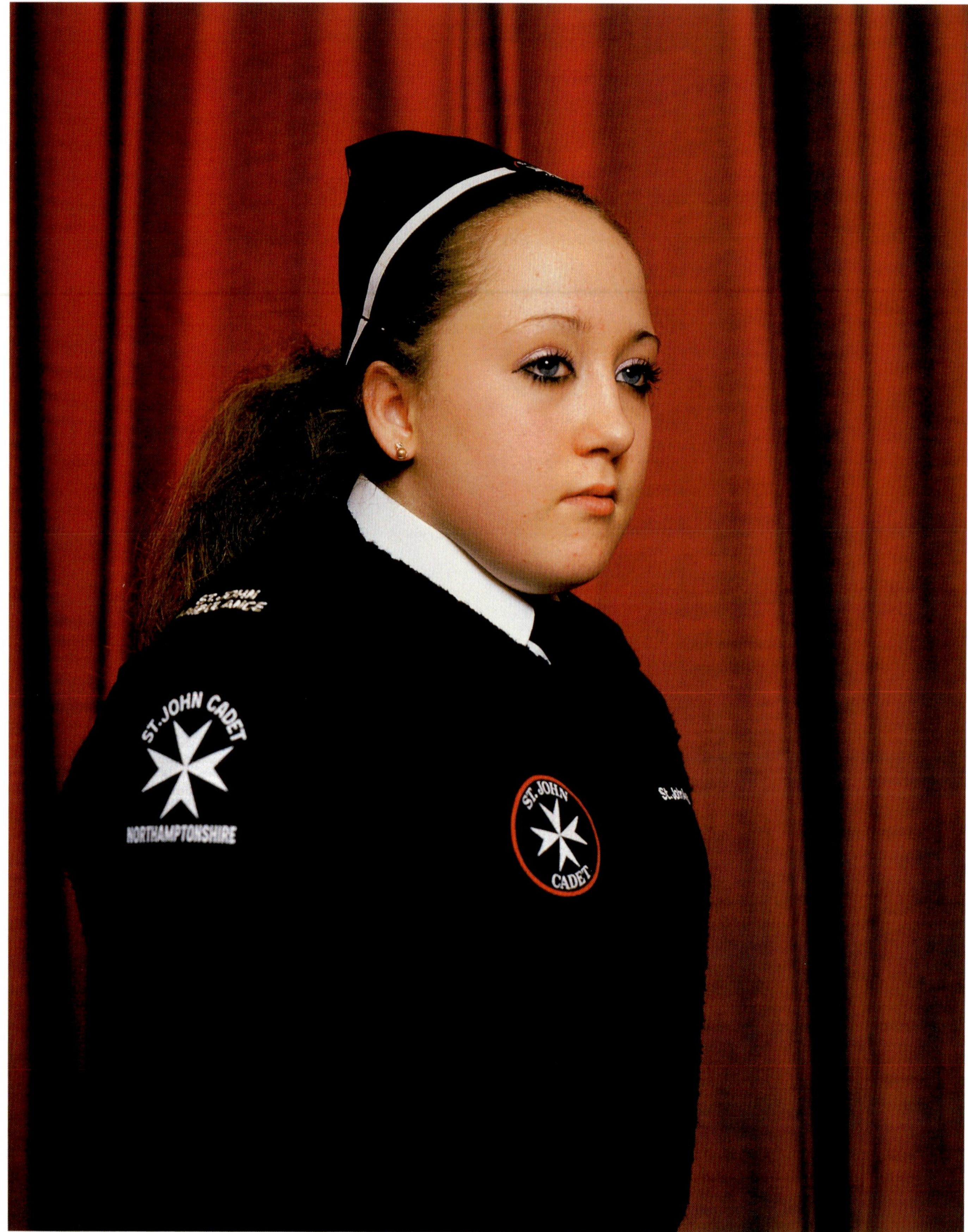

Zed Nelson

Kelley
from the series
Beauty Queens
June 2005

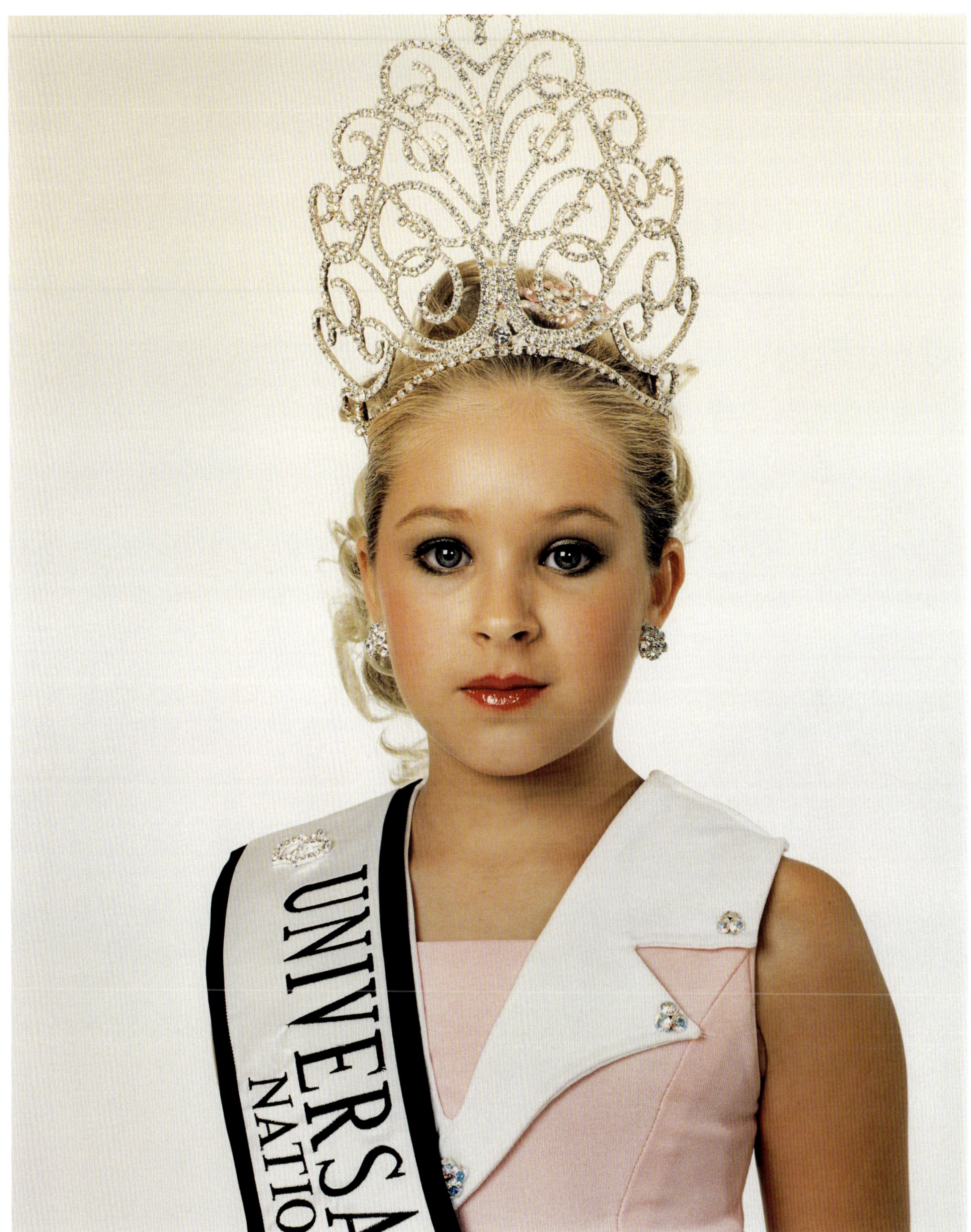

Tim MacPherson

Barber Shop
Pushka
January 2005

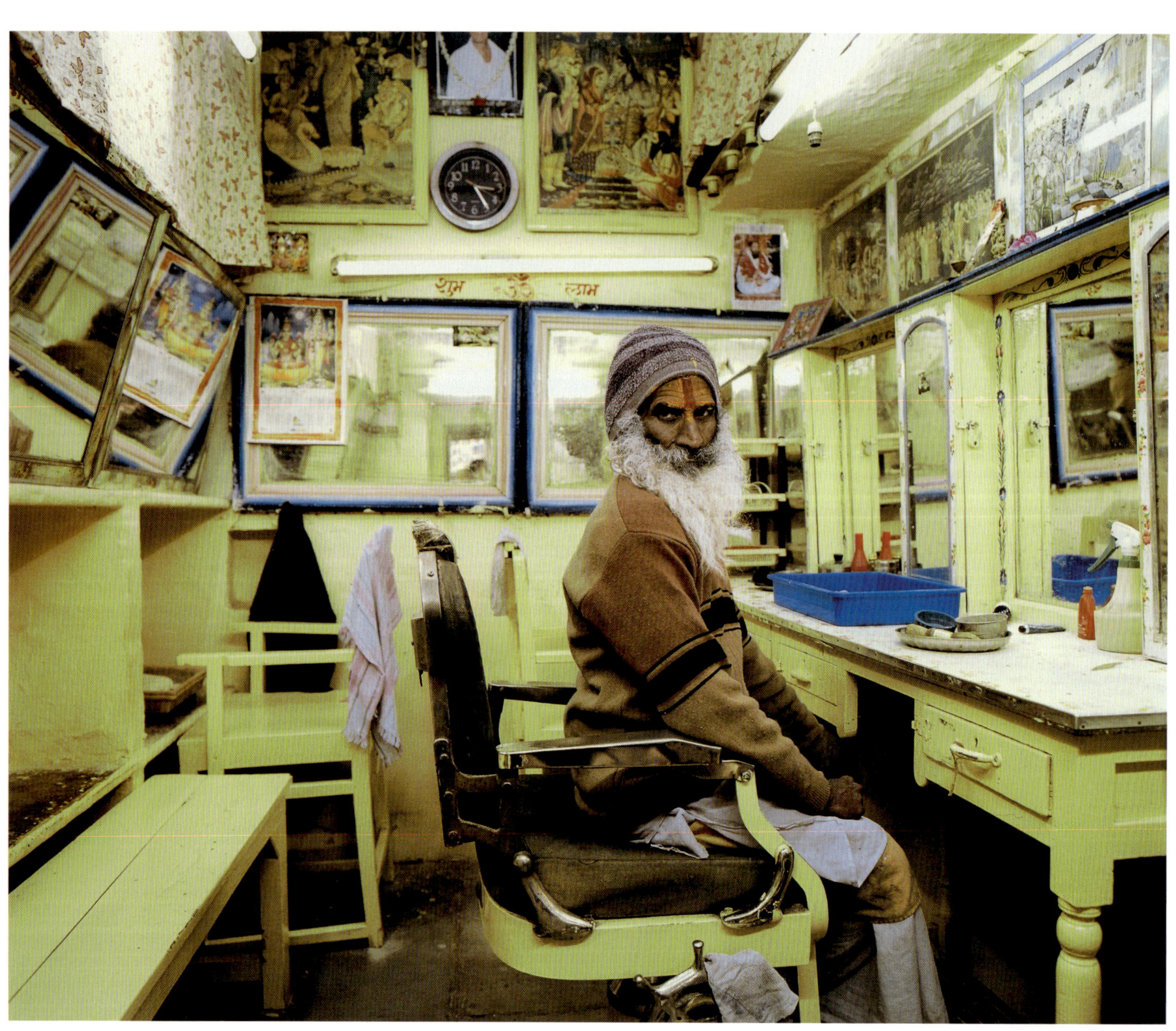

Robin George Stanley
Cat Man
June 2004

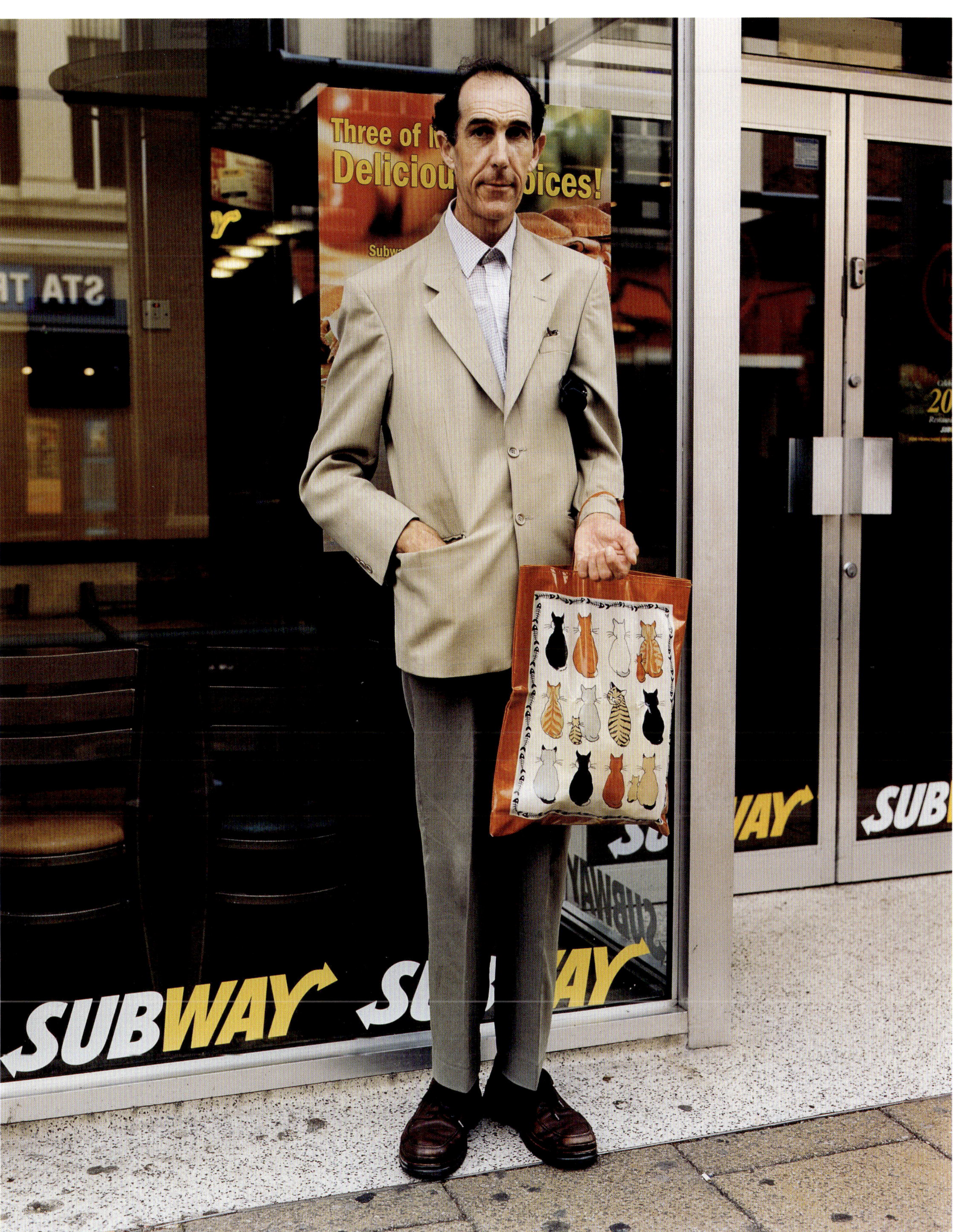

Steven Taylor

Annabel + Vicki
June 2005

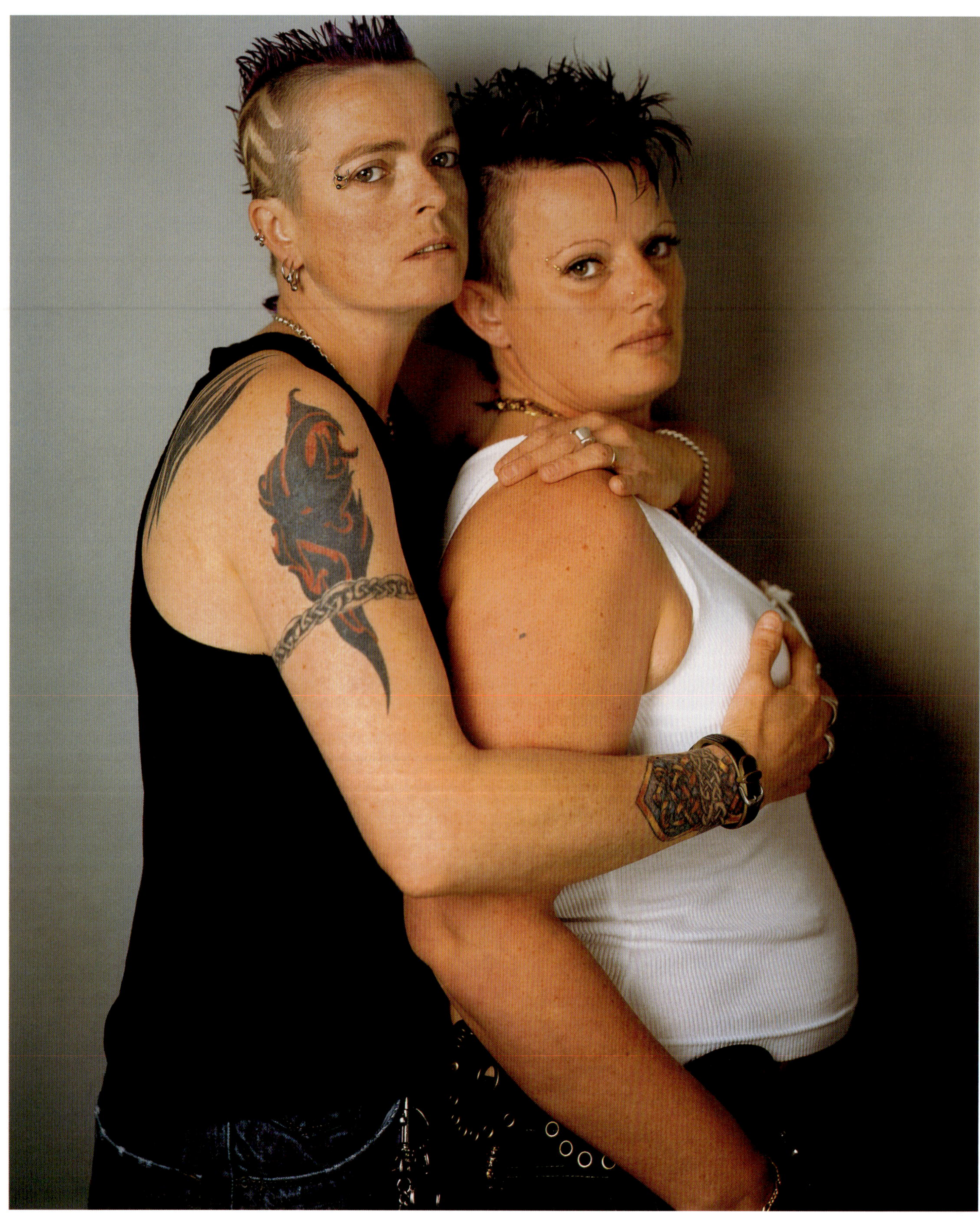

Dirk Lindner

Untitled *from the series* I am
December 2004

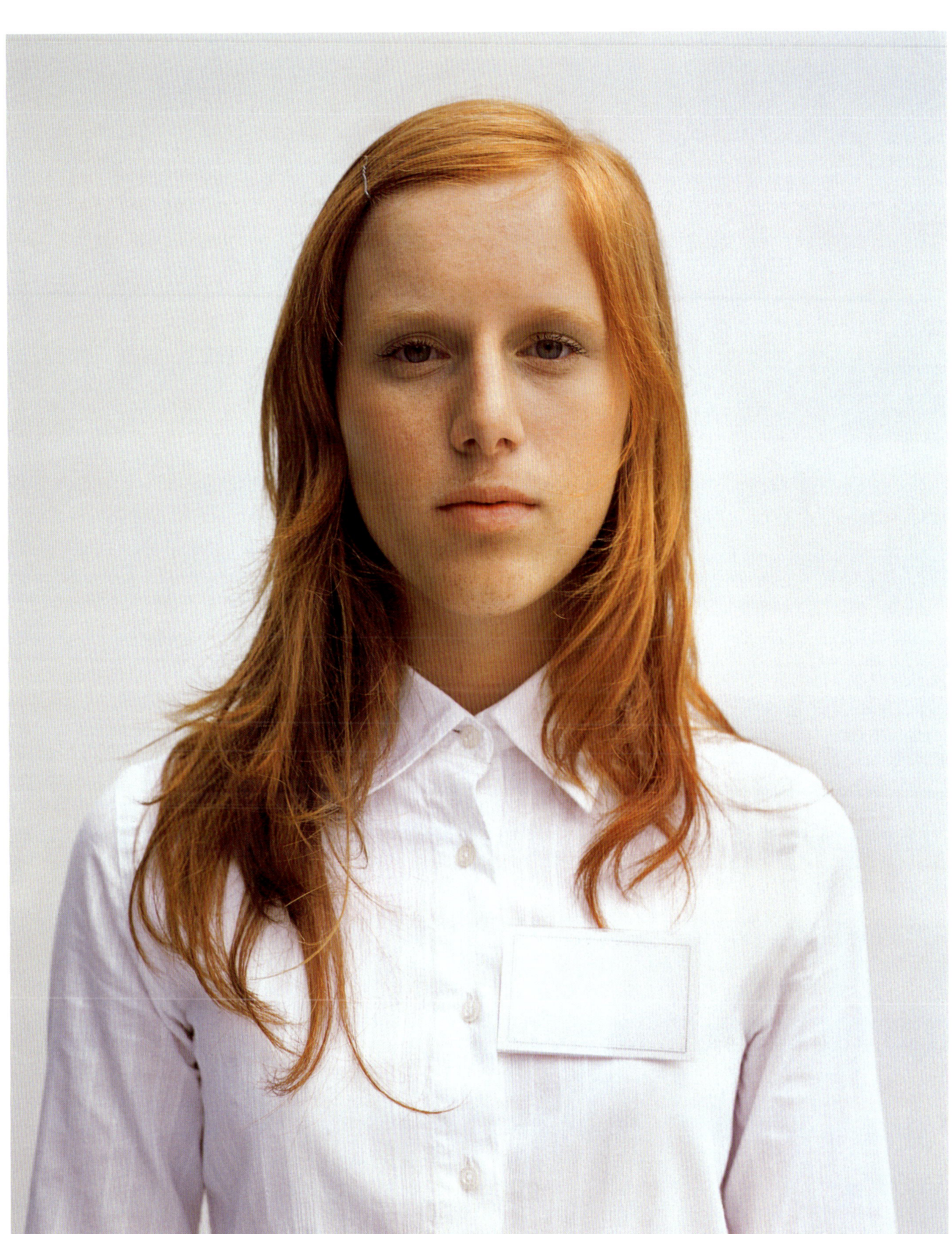

David Axelbank Dad and Dominique
August 2004

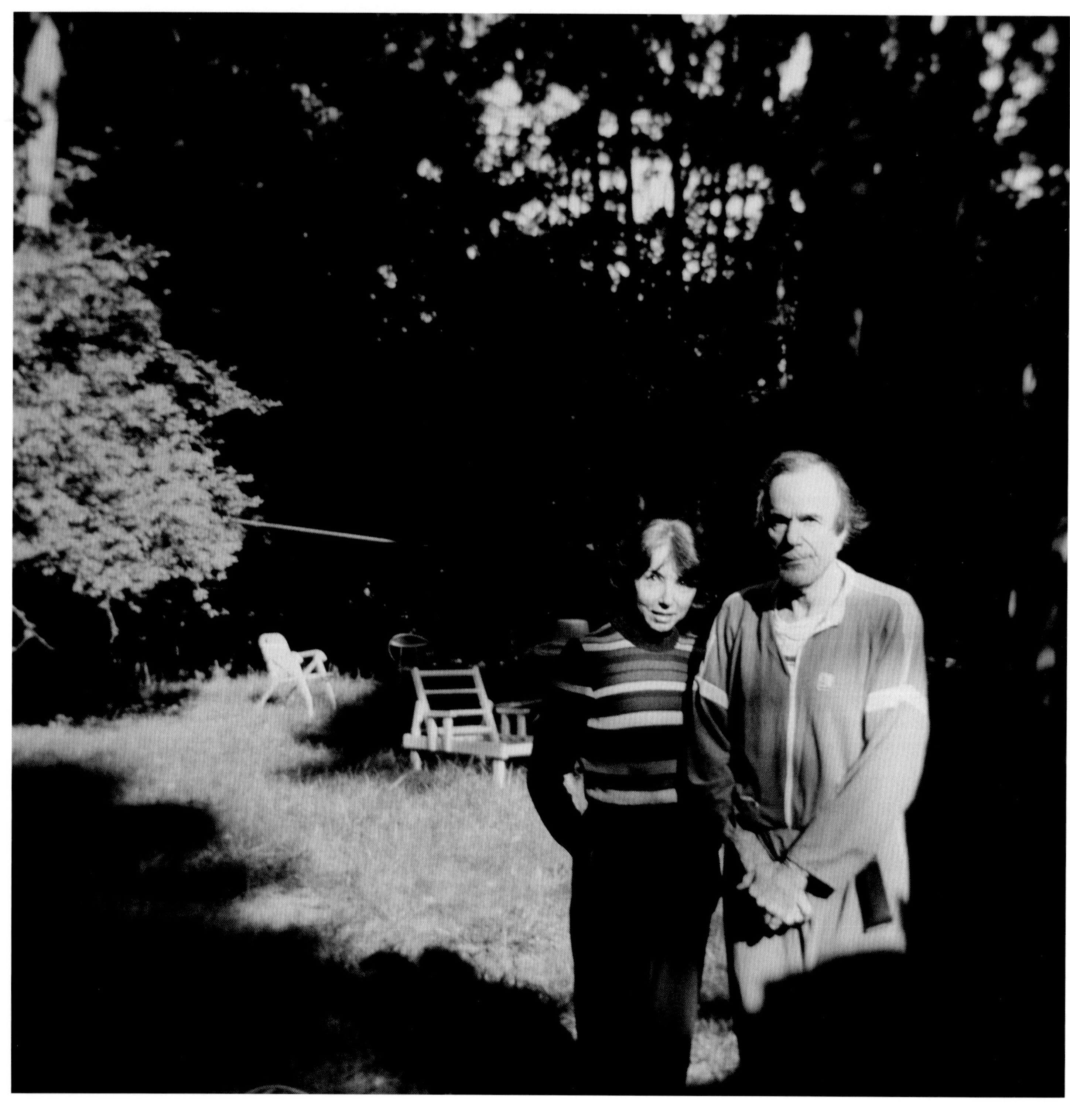

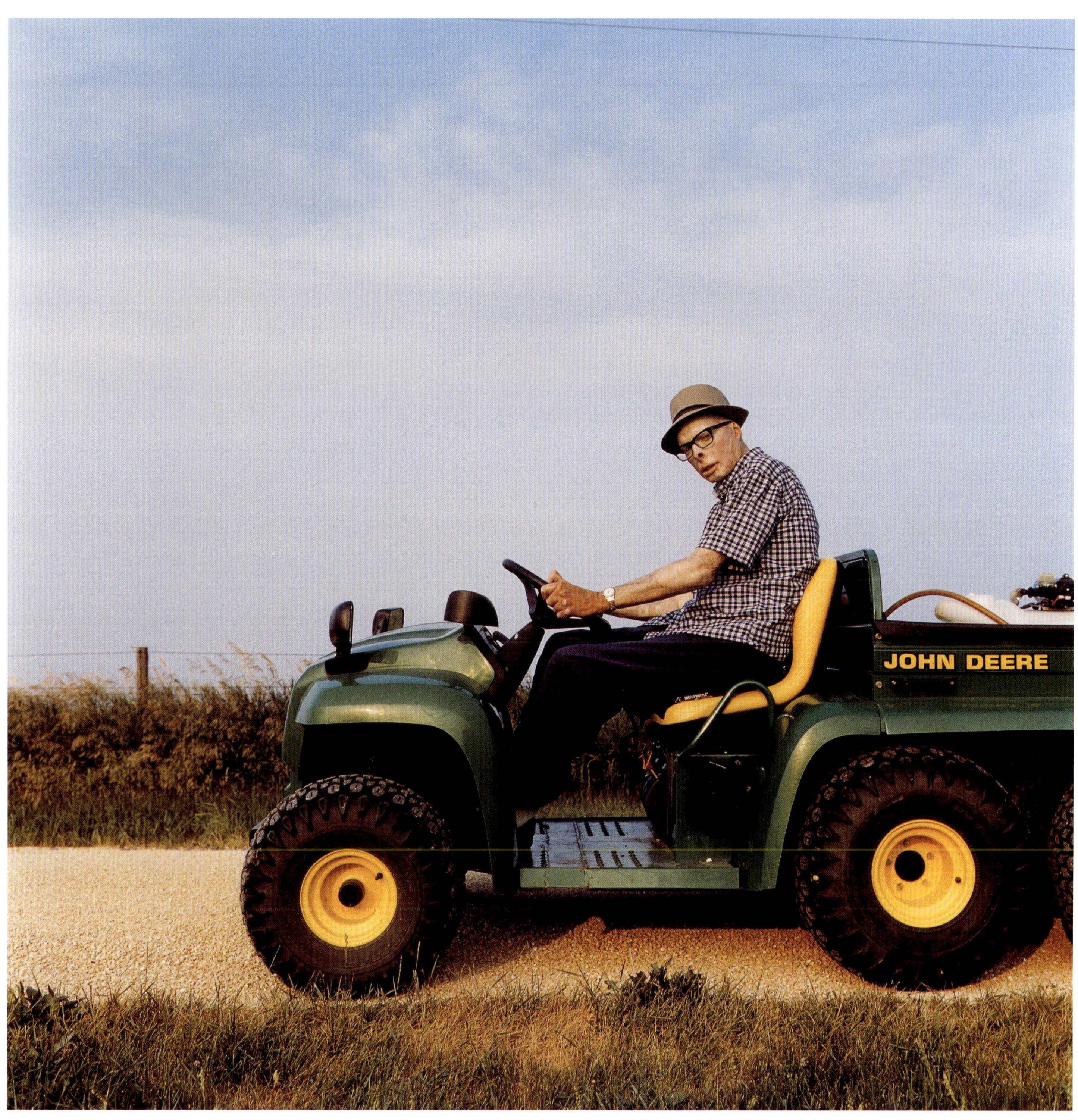
JOHN DEERE

Paul Plews **Untitled (Smithfield #2)** ***from the series*** **The Morning After** September 2004

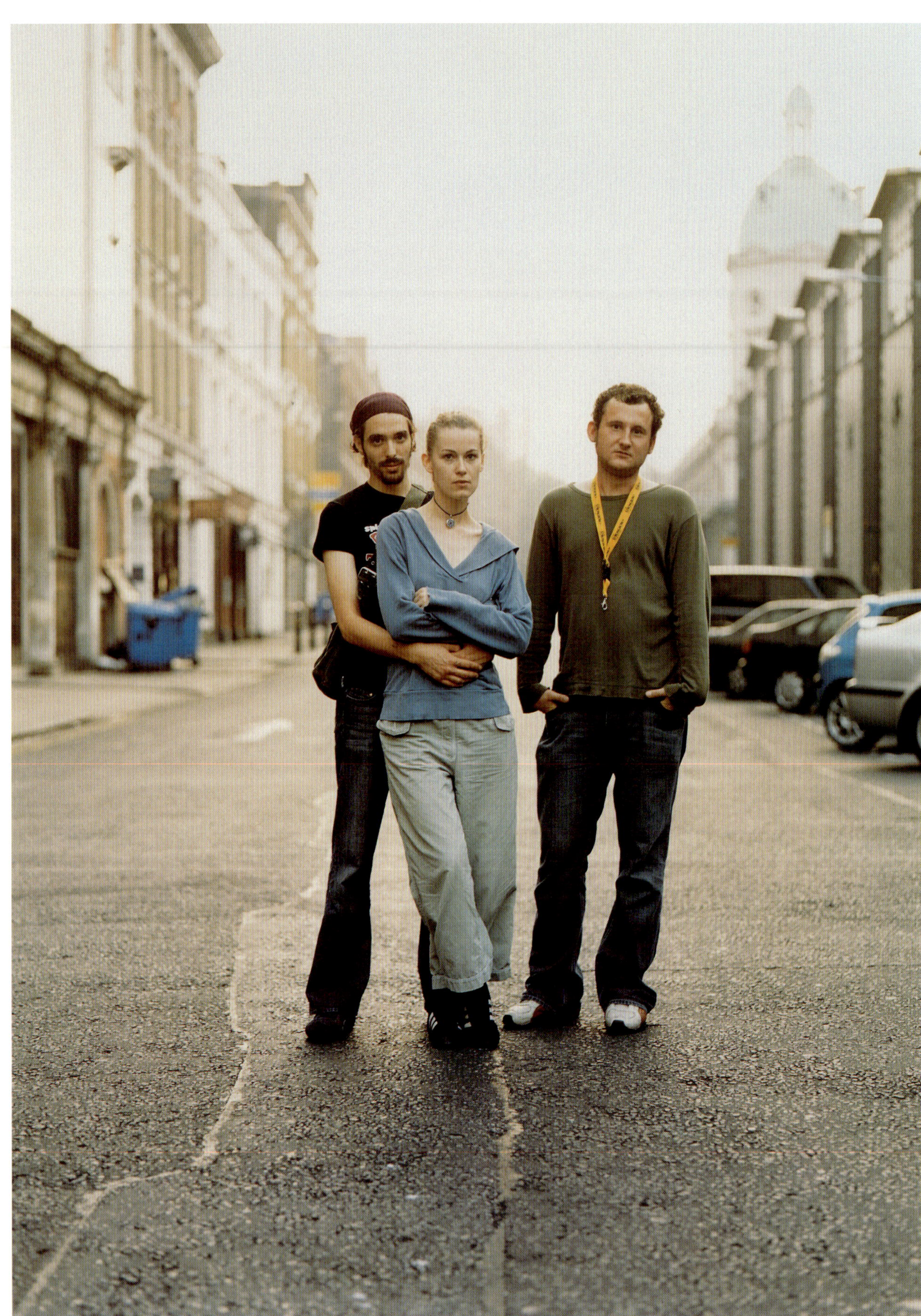

David Stewart

Thomas Family
from the series
Relations
February 2005

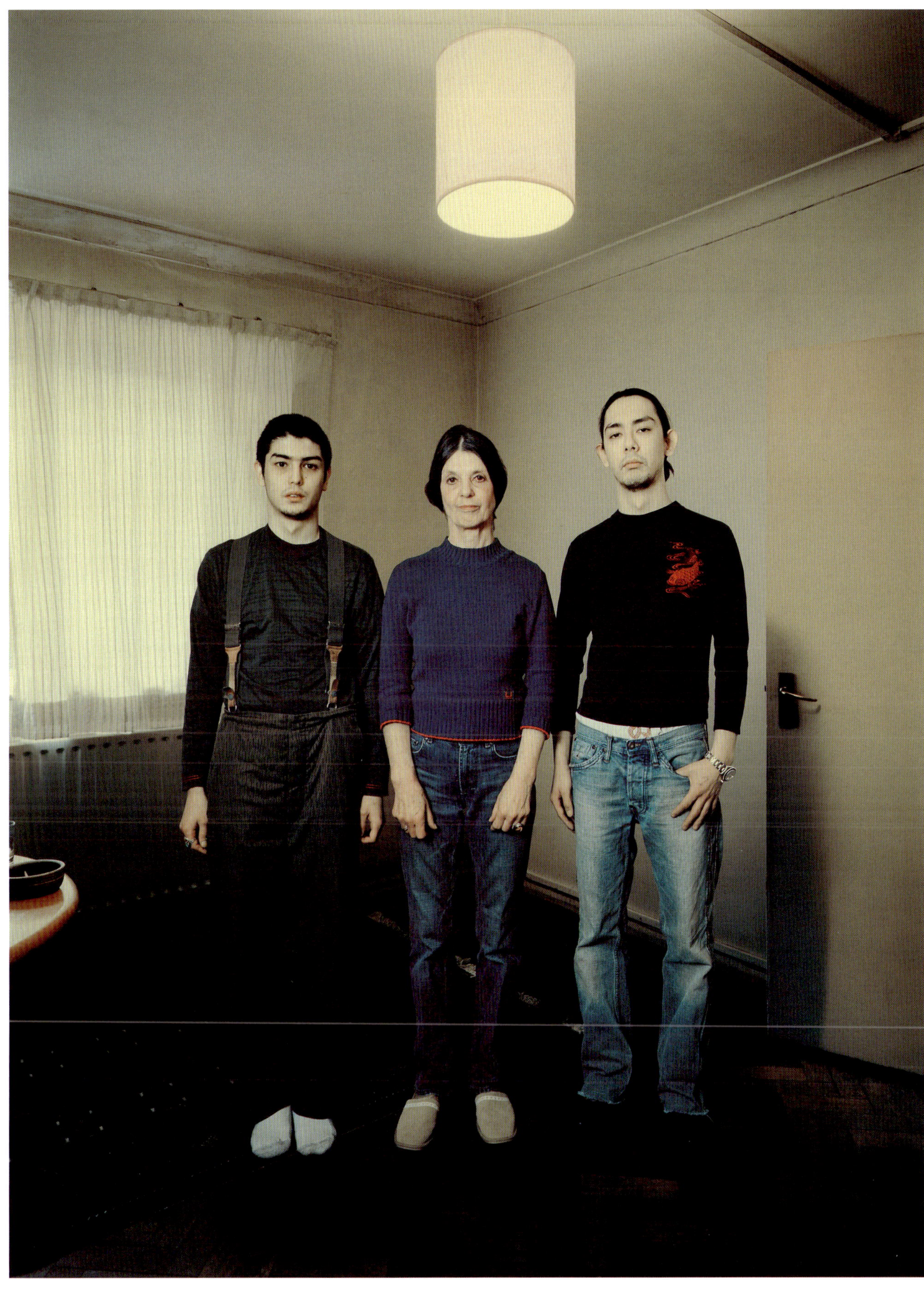

Zsofia Molnar

Charlie
February 2005

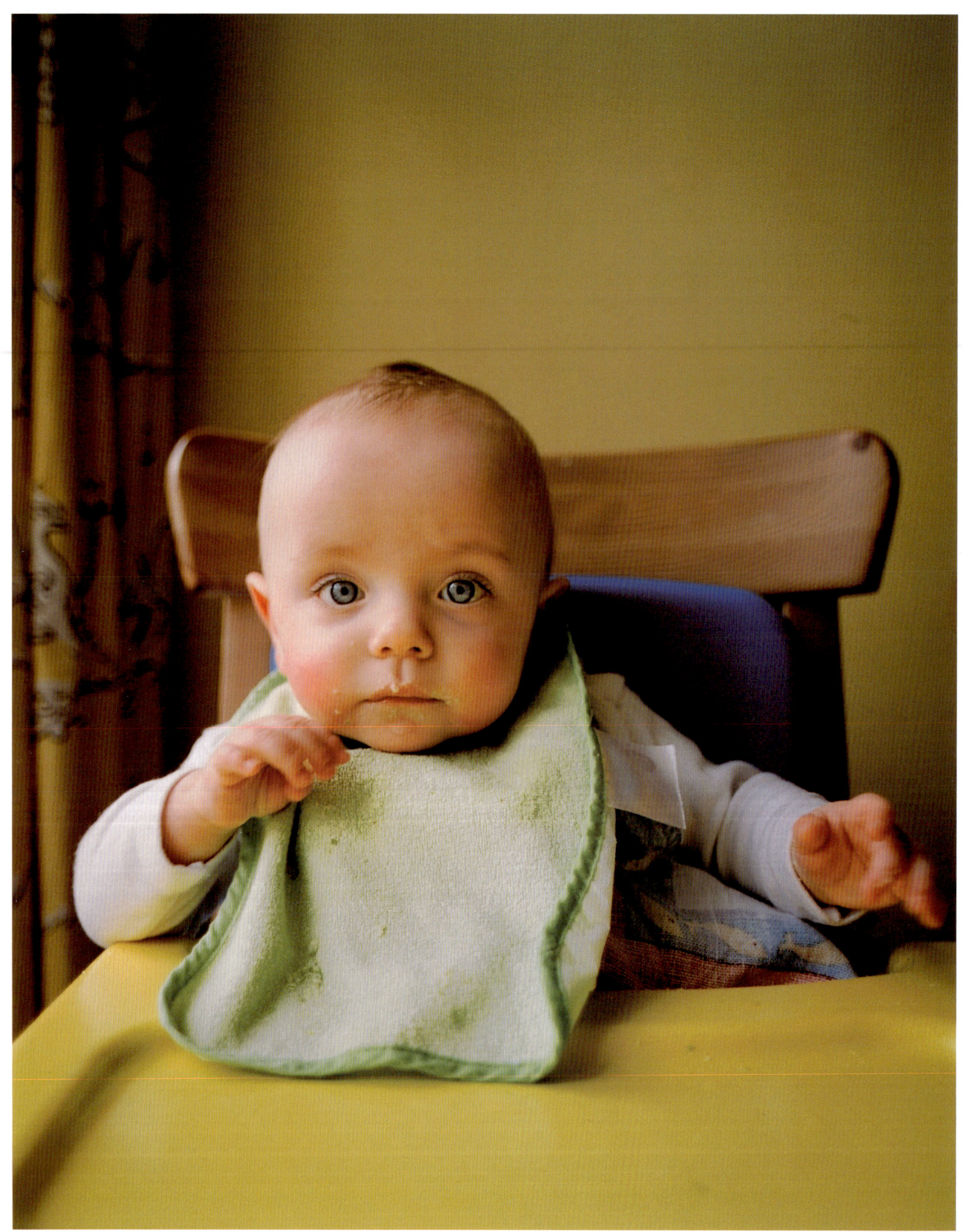

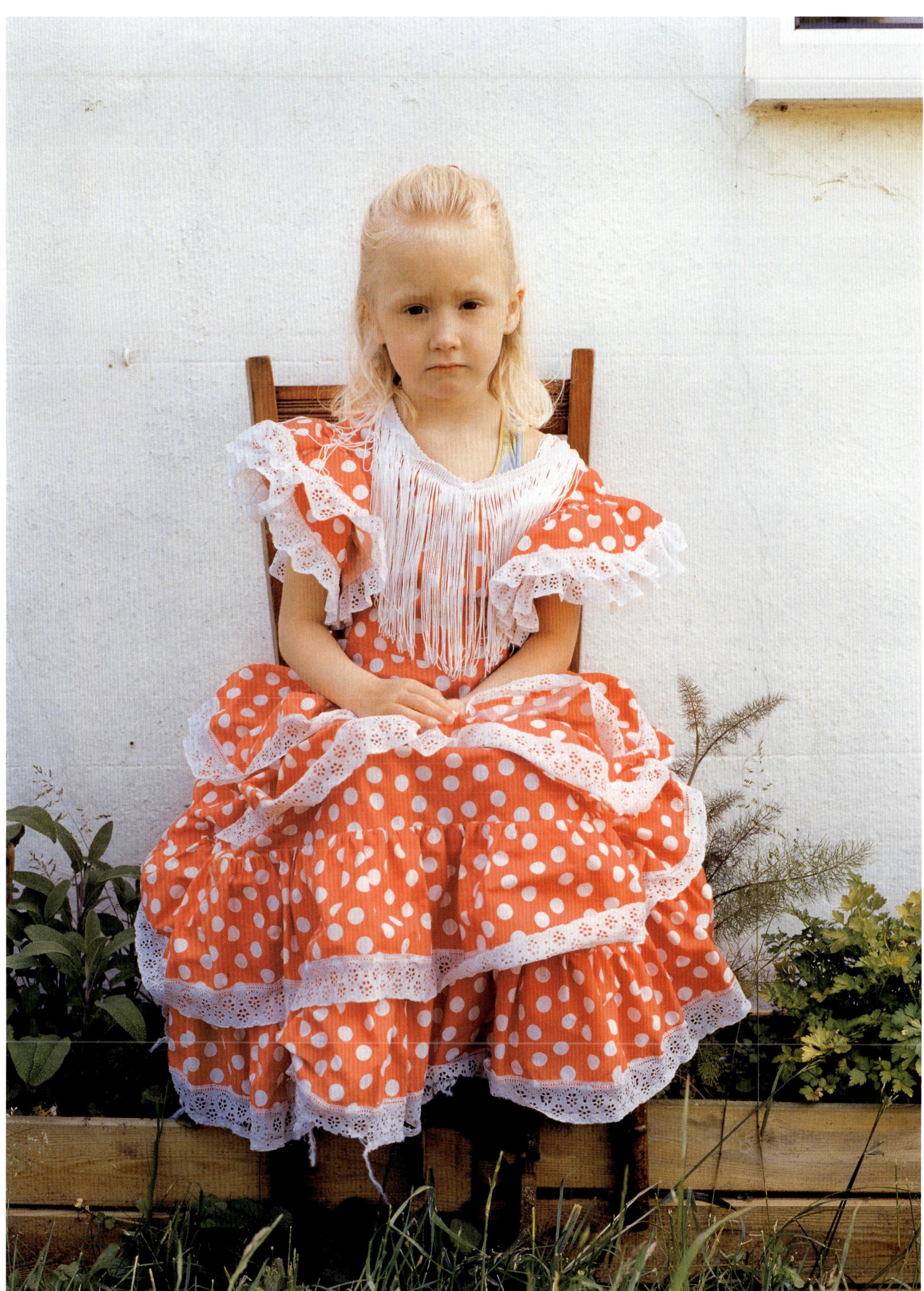

Giles Godwin

(In the Bride's Room)
Jeeta and Her Friends
from the series Bilga
April 2005

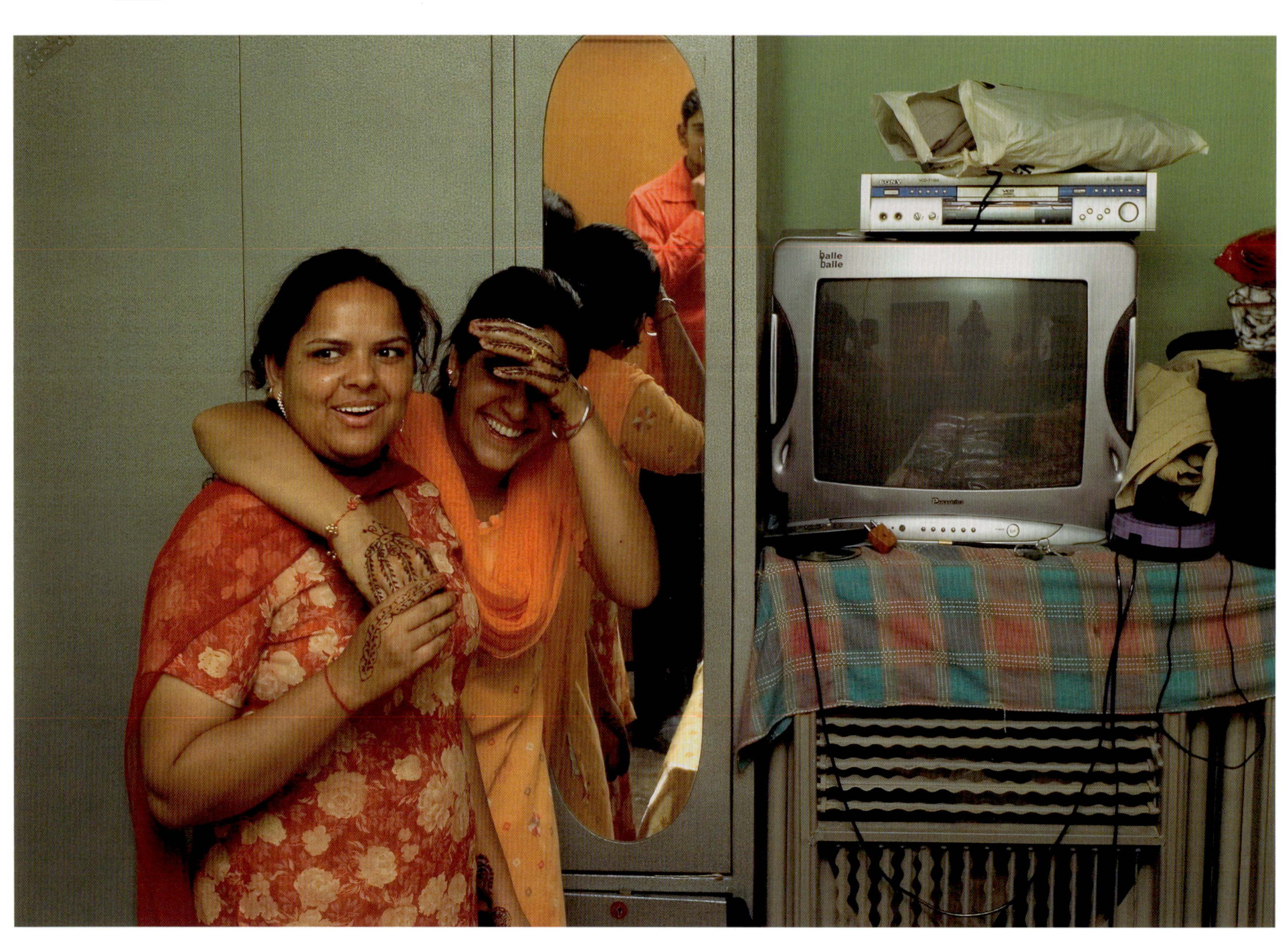

Jonathan
Torgovnik

Nozibele Mditshwa
and Daughter
July 2004

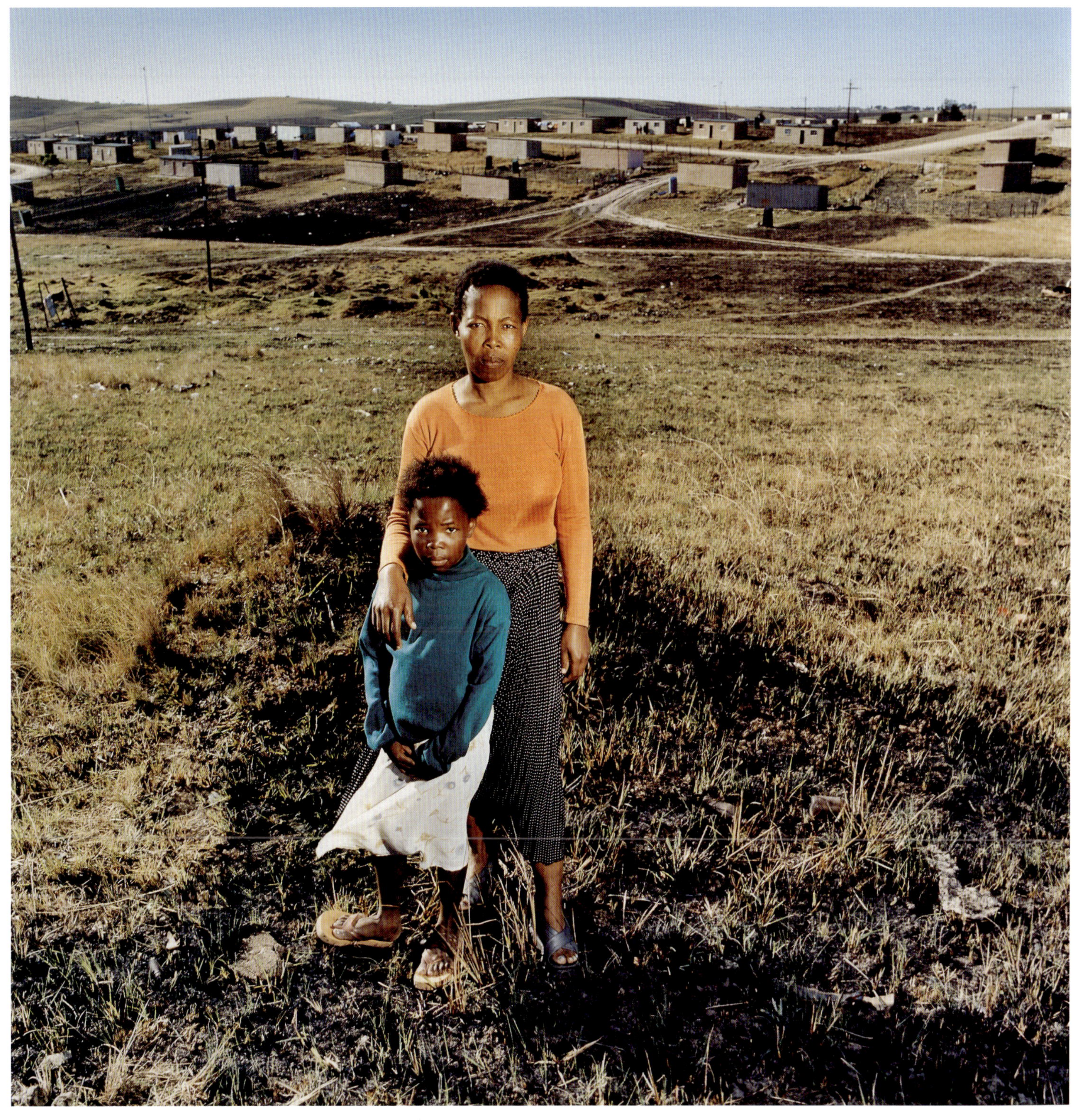

Jo Broughton

Pete Doherty
May 2005

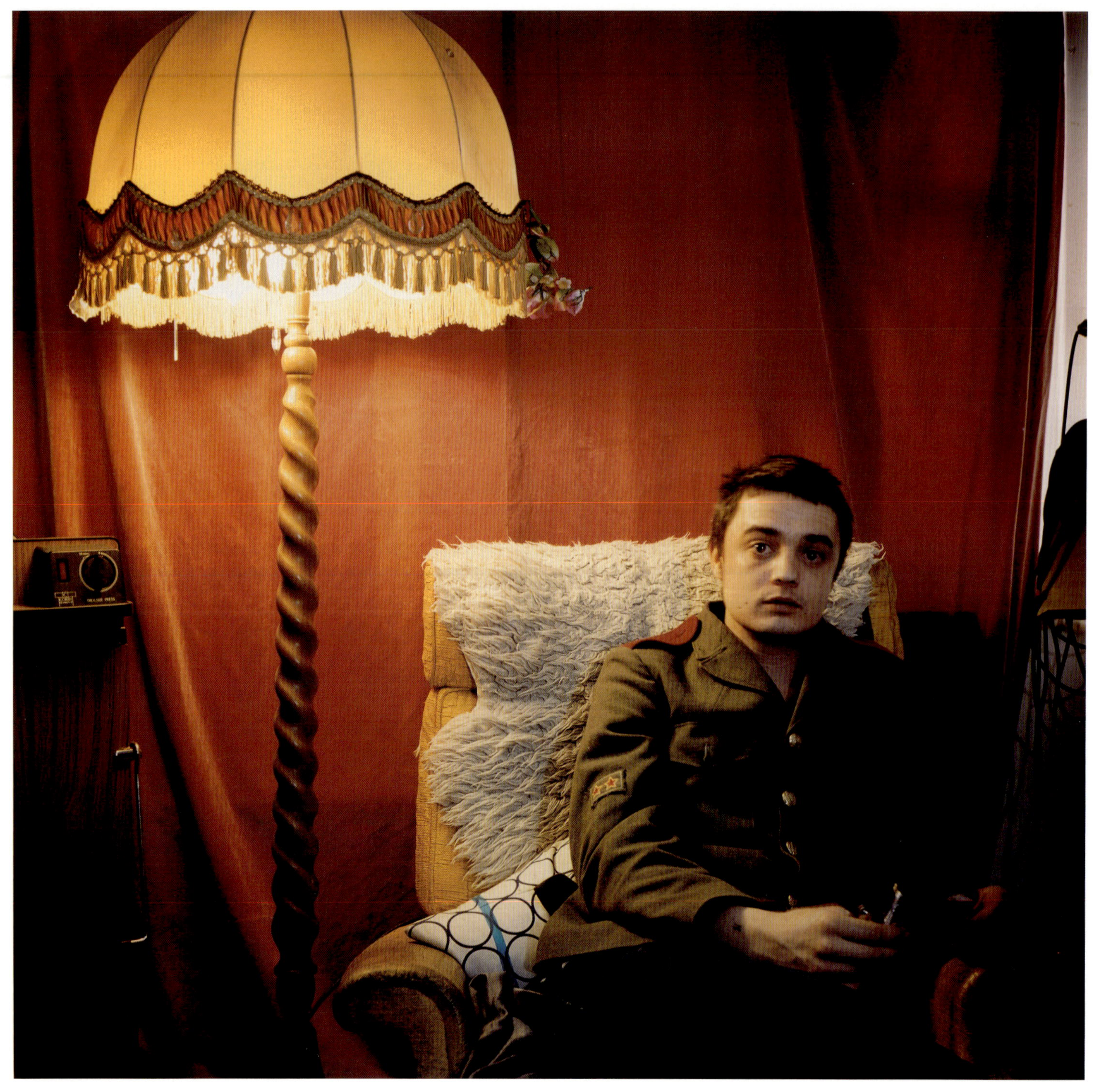

Michal Chelbin Young Cadets
September 2004

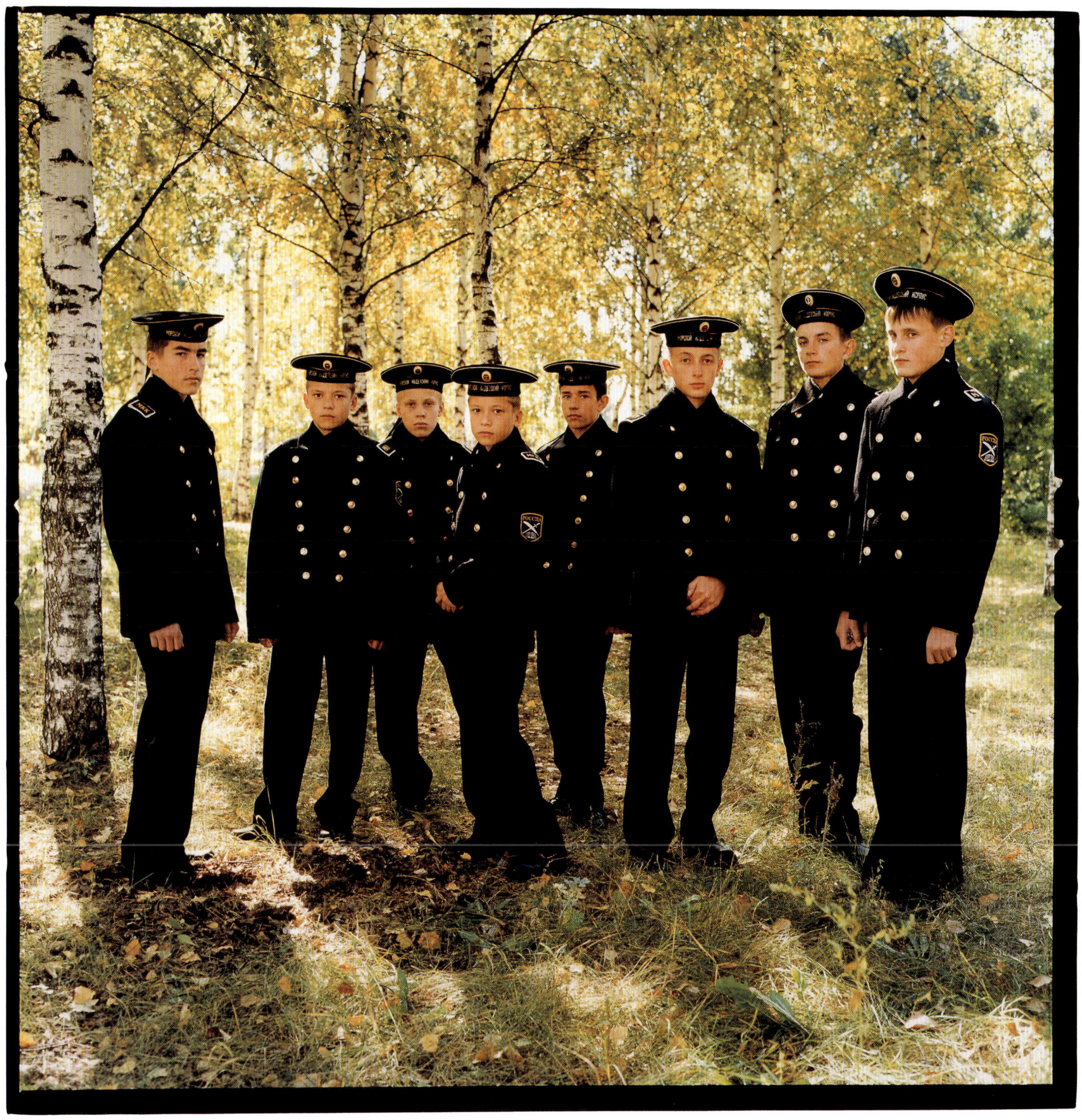

Gered Mankowitz

The Beach Family
from the series
Portrait of St Lucia
June 2004

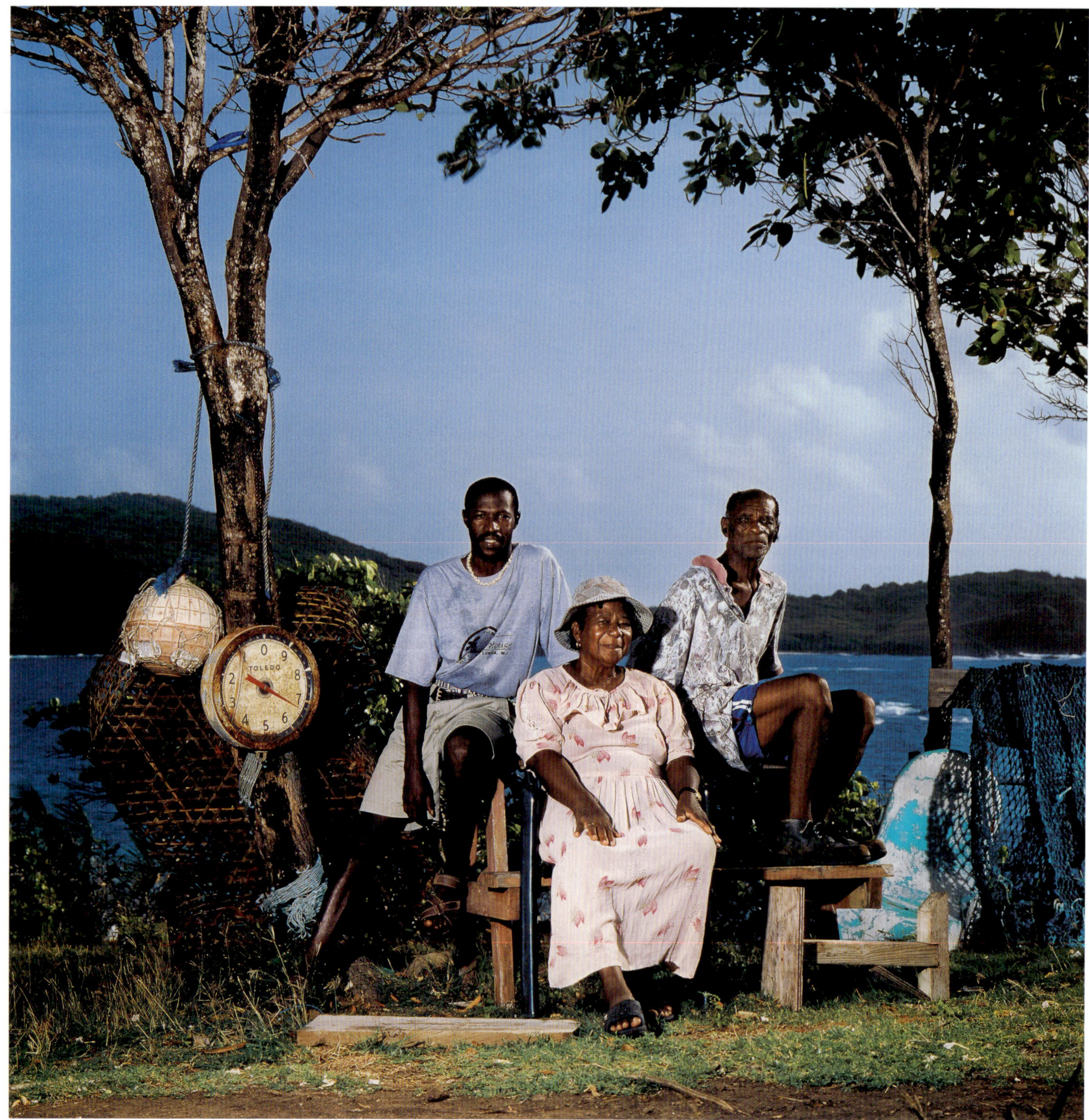

David Modell

Couple at Garden Centre, Reading
March 2005

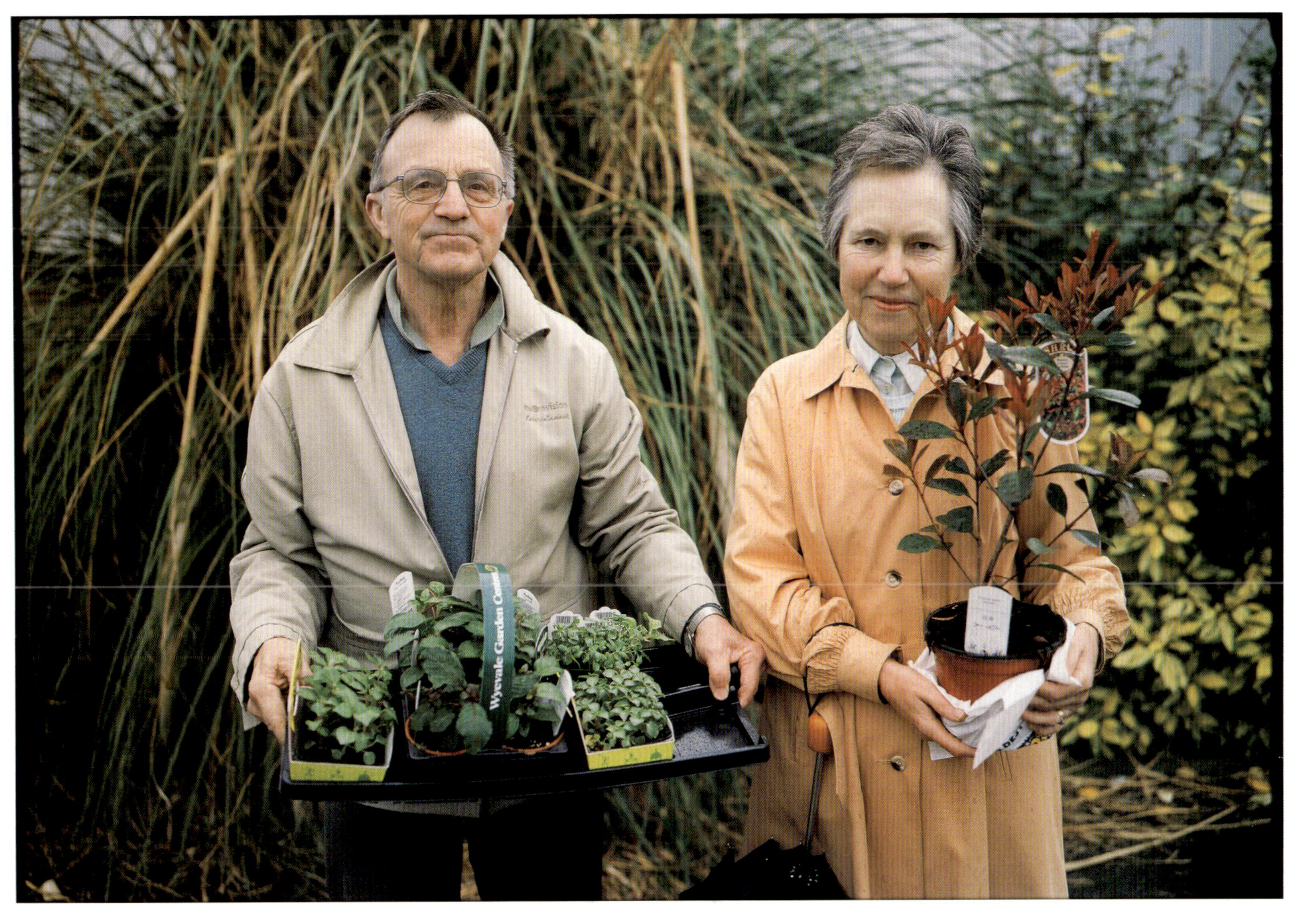

Tara Moore

Coming Home
July 2005

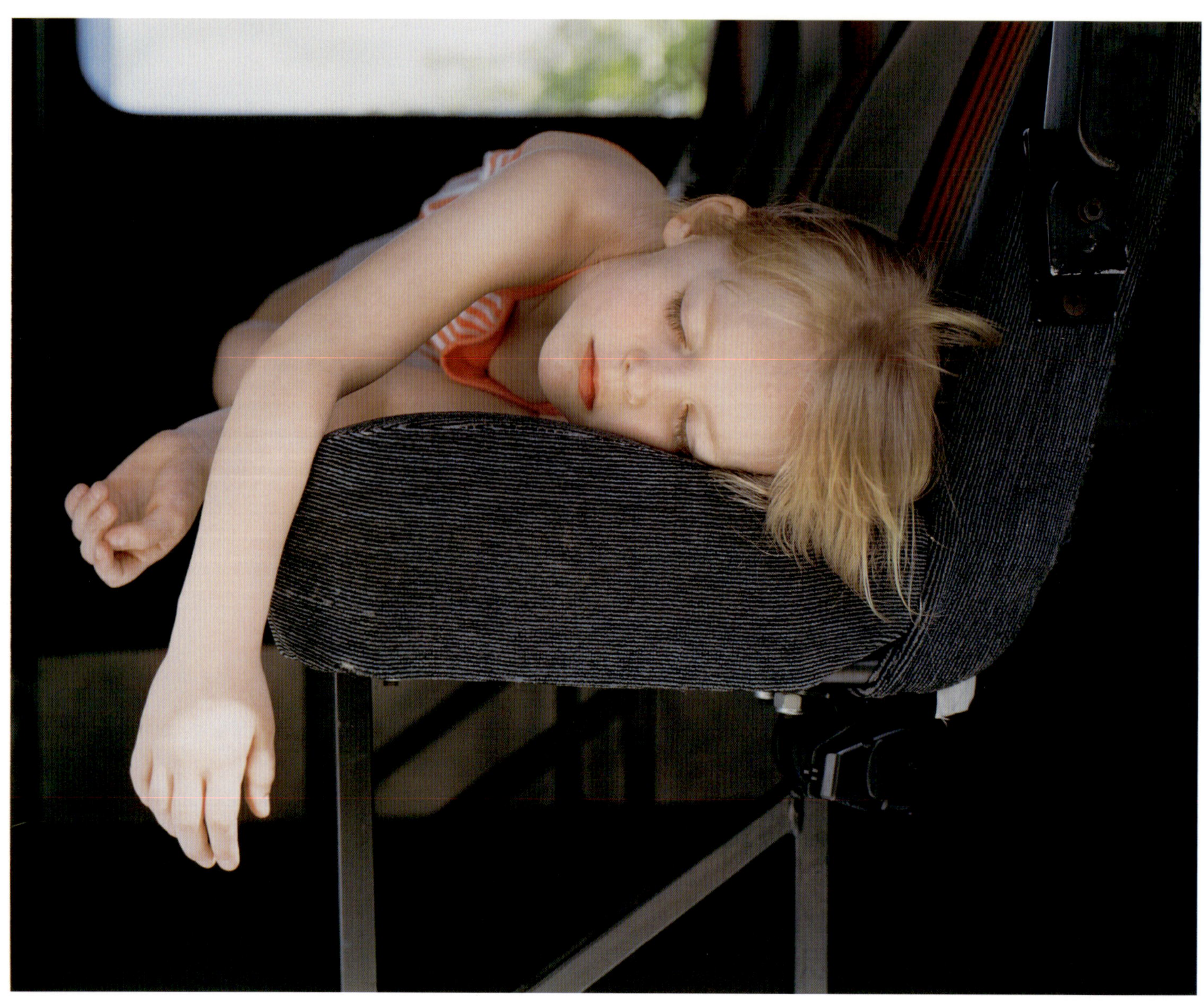

James
Yeats-Brown

Ella, Age 7, 2005
June 2005

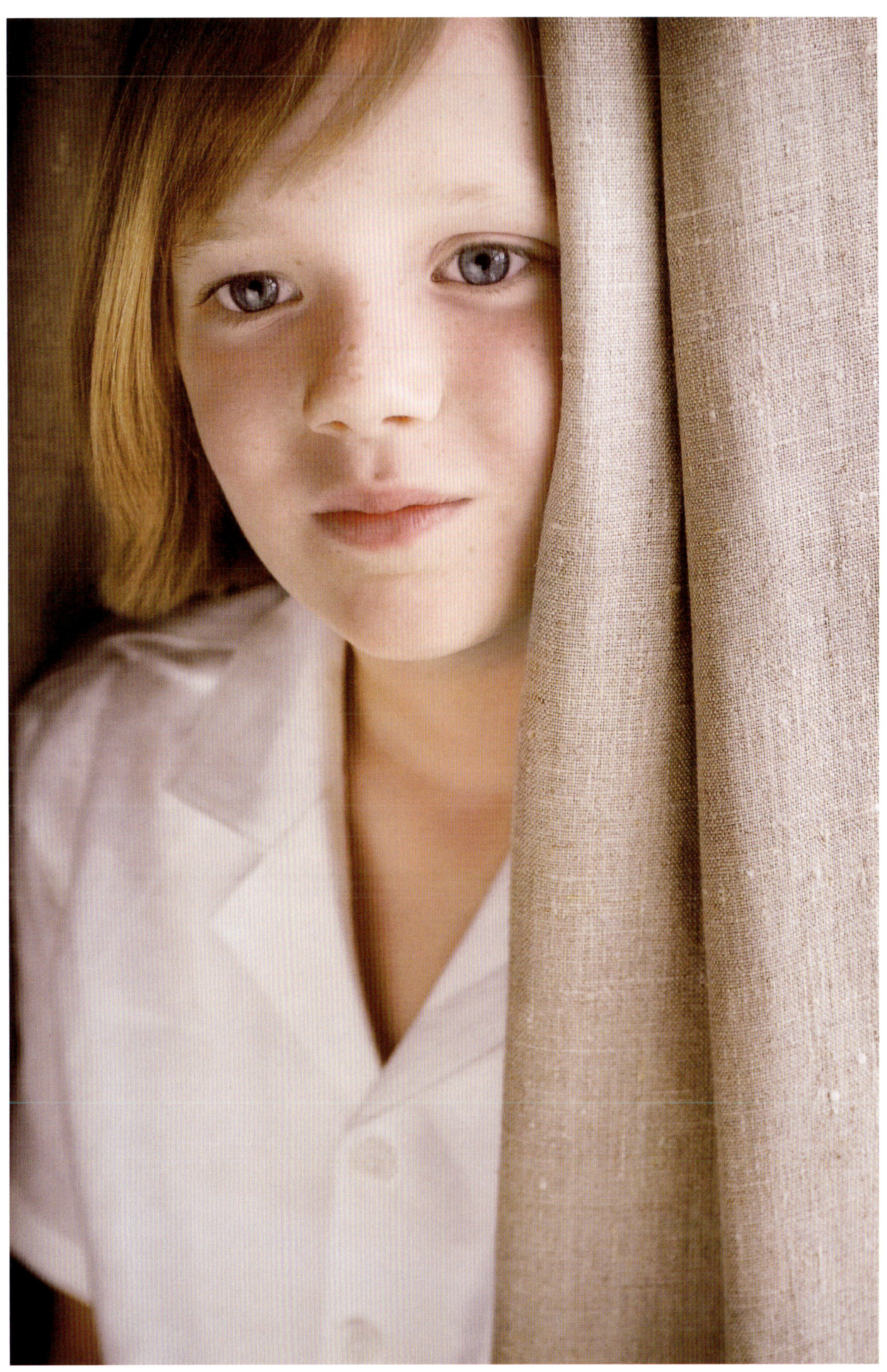

Southern Belle
October 2004

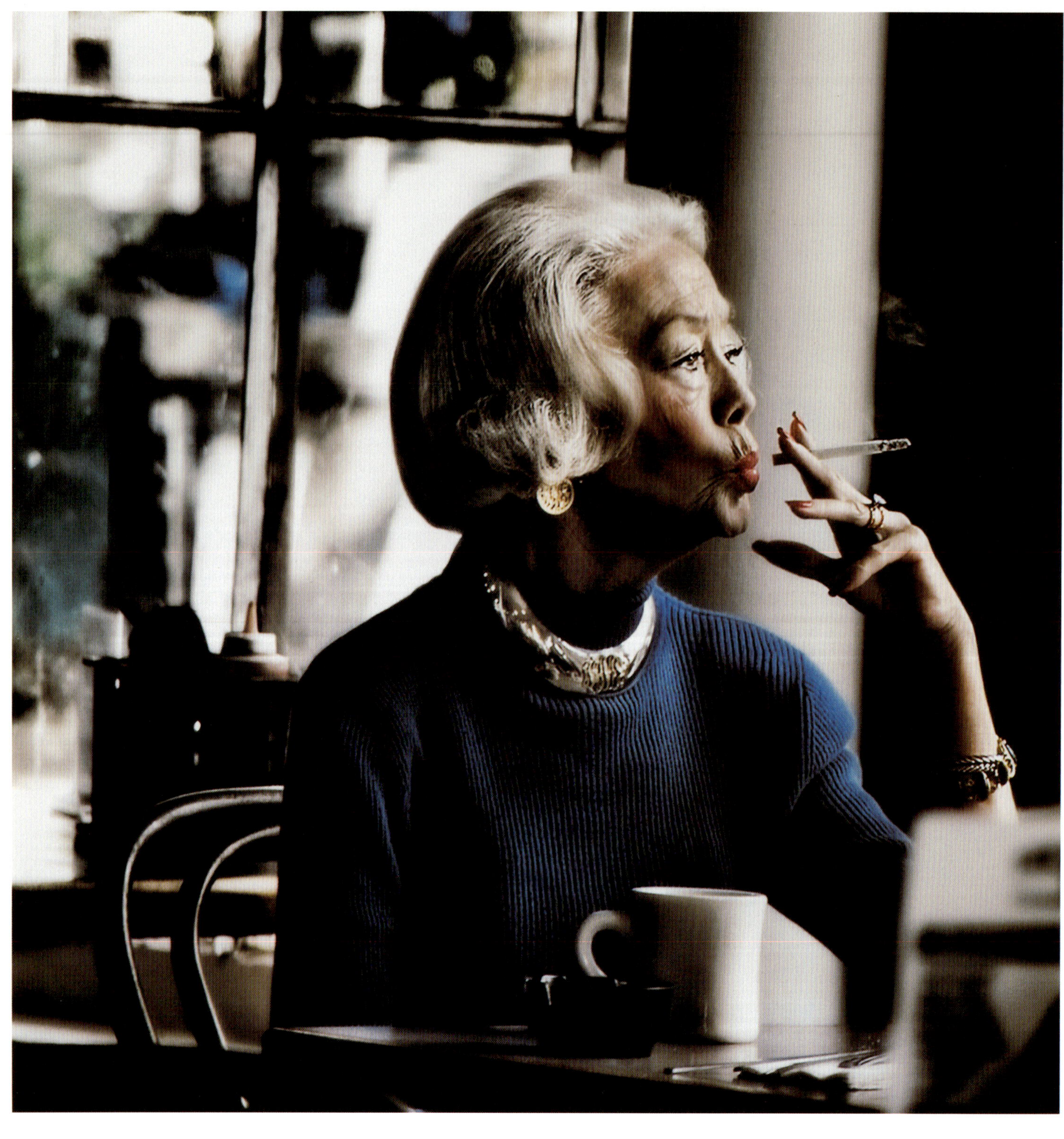

Rory Carnegie

Ray @ Carpet Right
from the series
Botley Rd/The Invisibles
July 2005

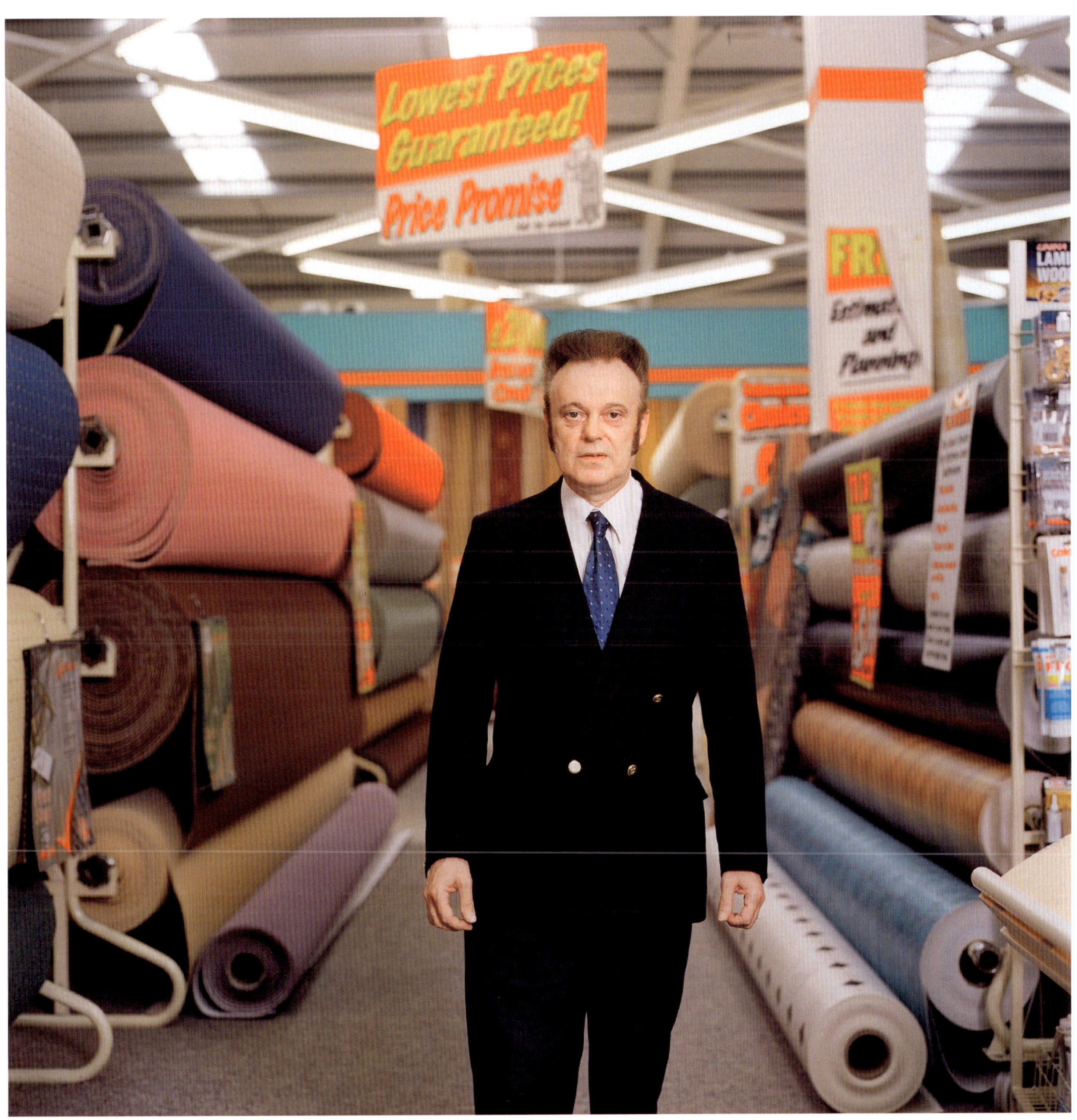

Kelvin Murray

Man Eating Sandwich
October 2004

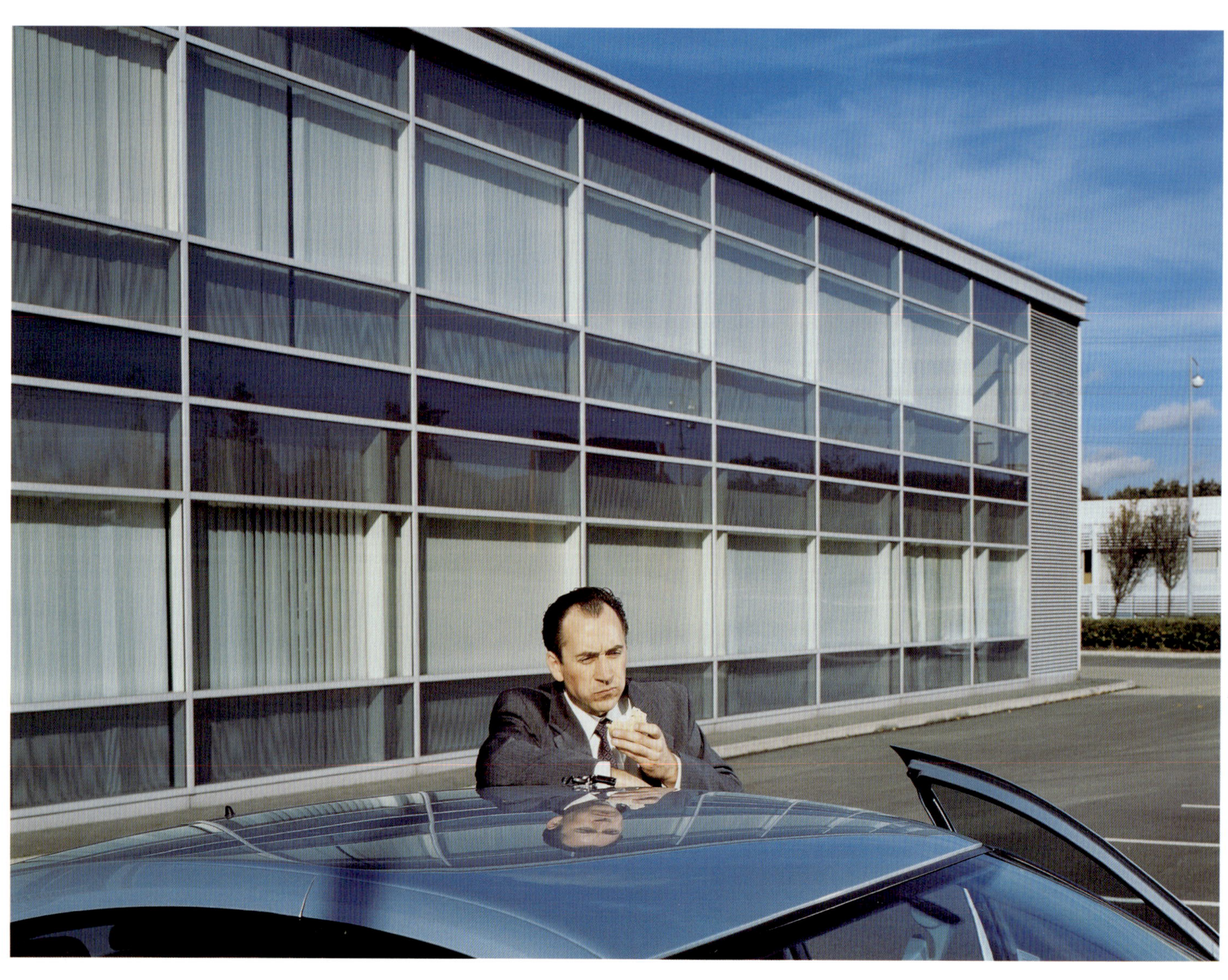

Paul Brooking

Shiram Waiting for Breakfast
July 2005

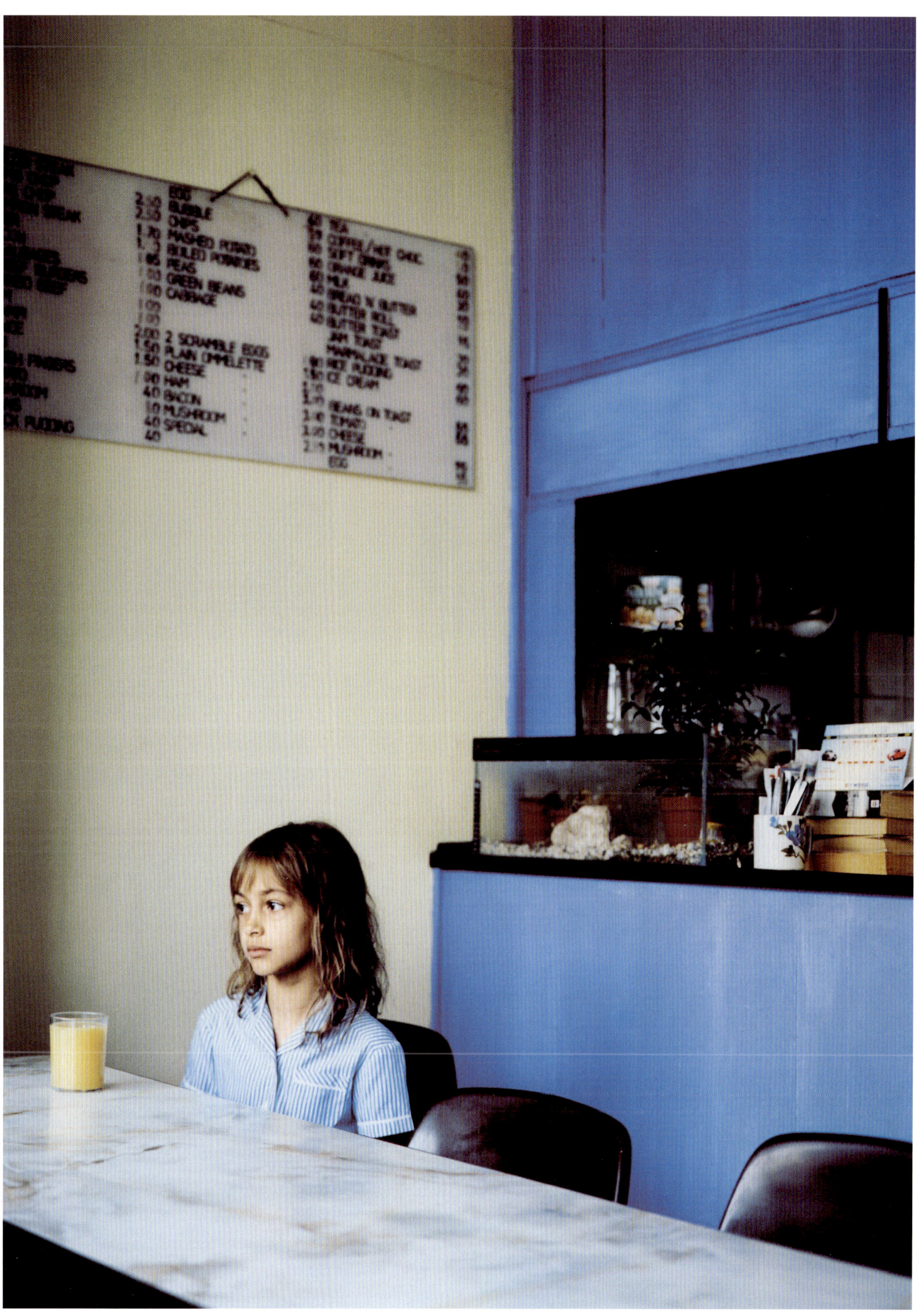

Lottie Davies

Cook, Meno Akwena, Botswana
June 2005

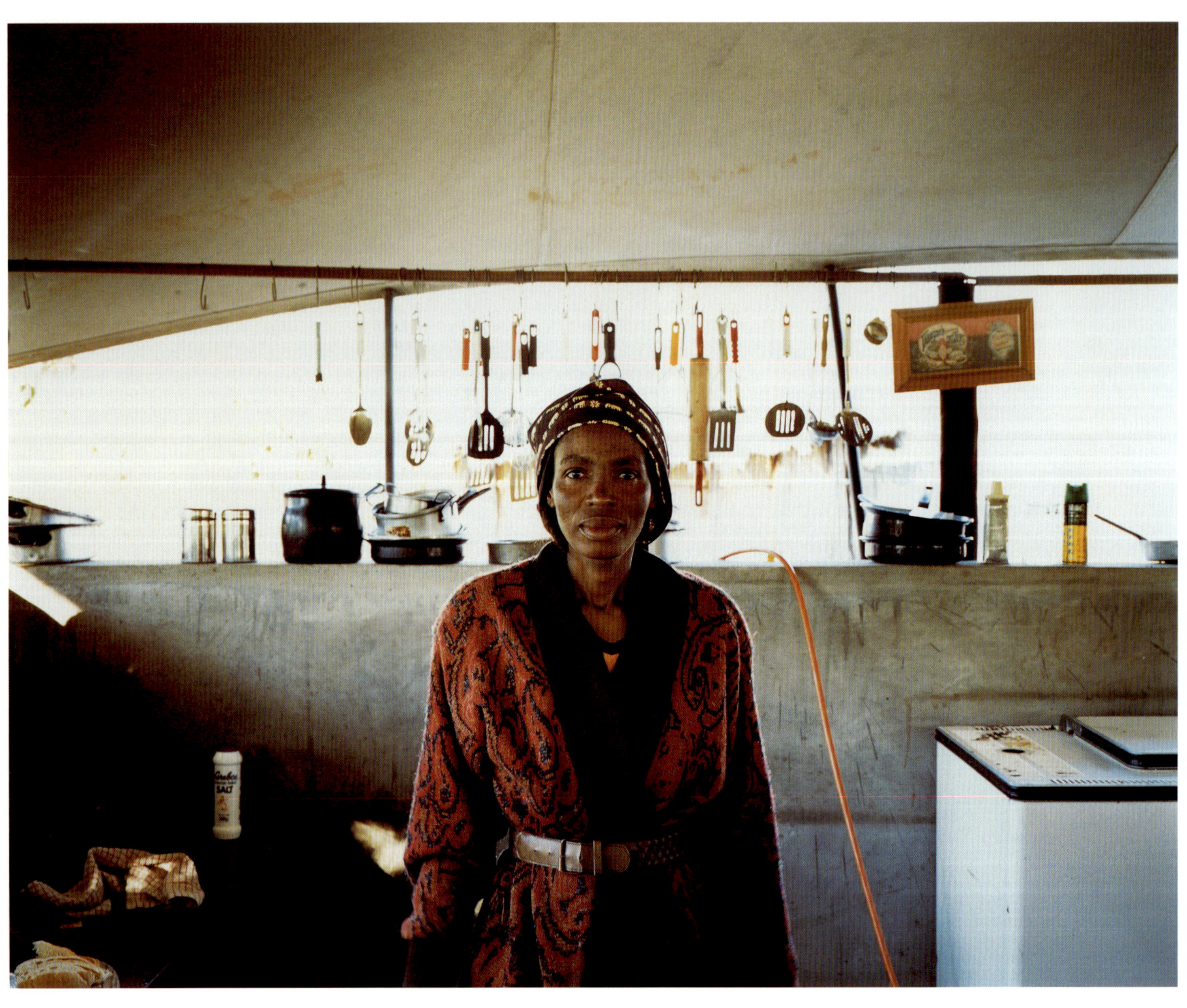

Hannah Illsley

Helen Going On Holiday to Harris
from the series
Over The Sea
April 2005

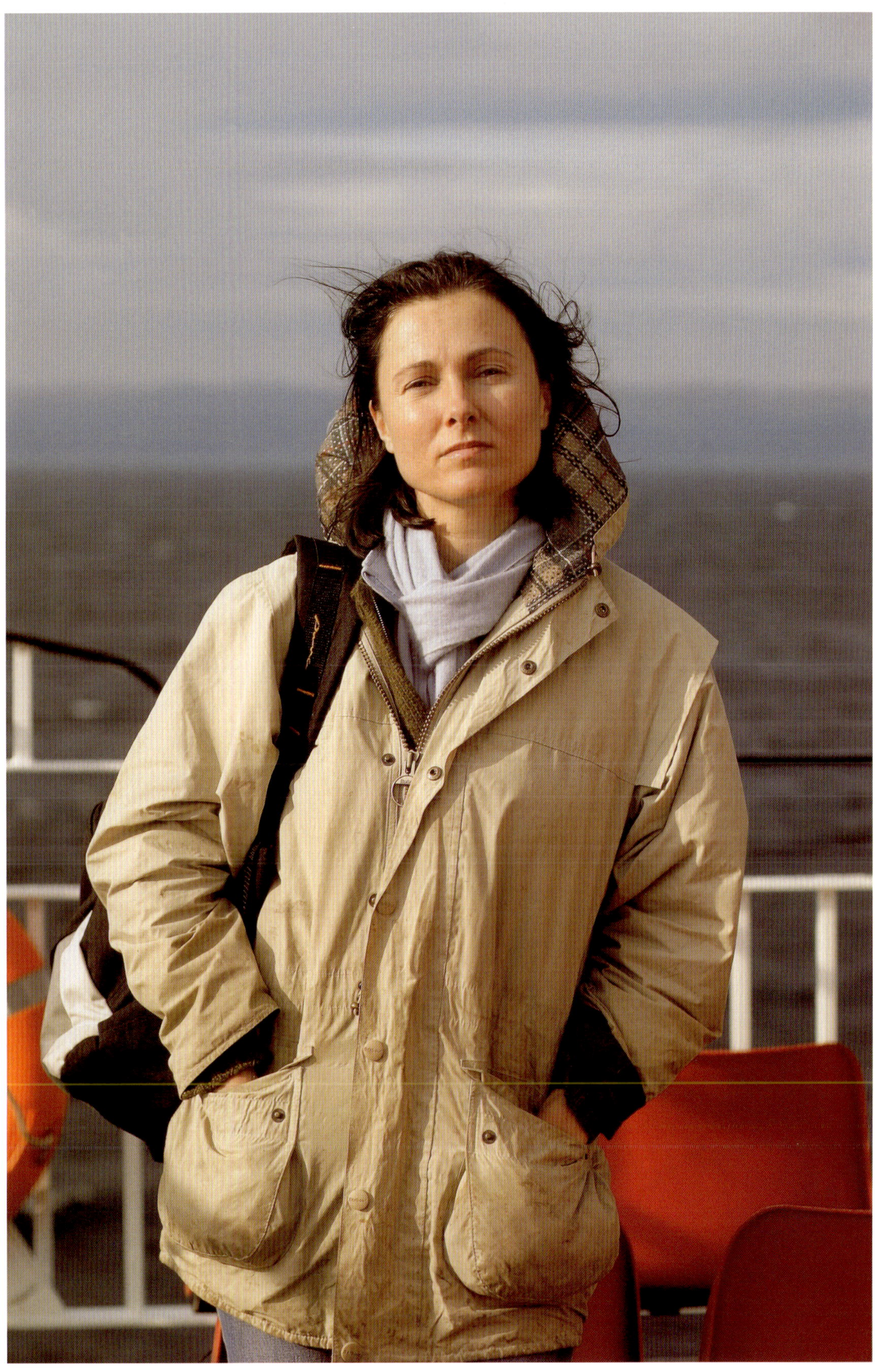

Richard Ansett

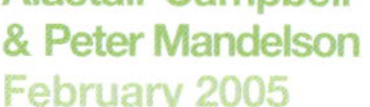

Alastair Campbell
& Peter Mandelson
February 2005

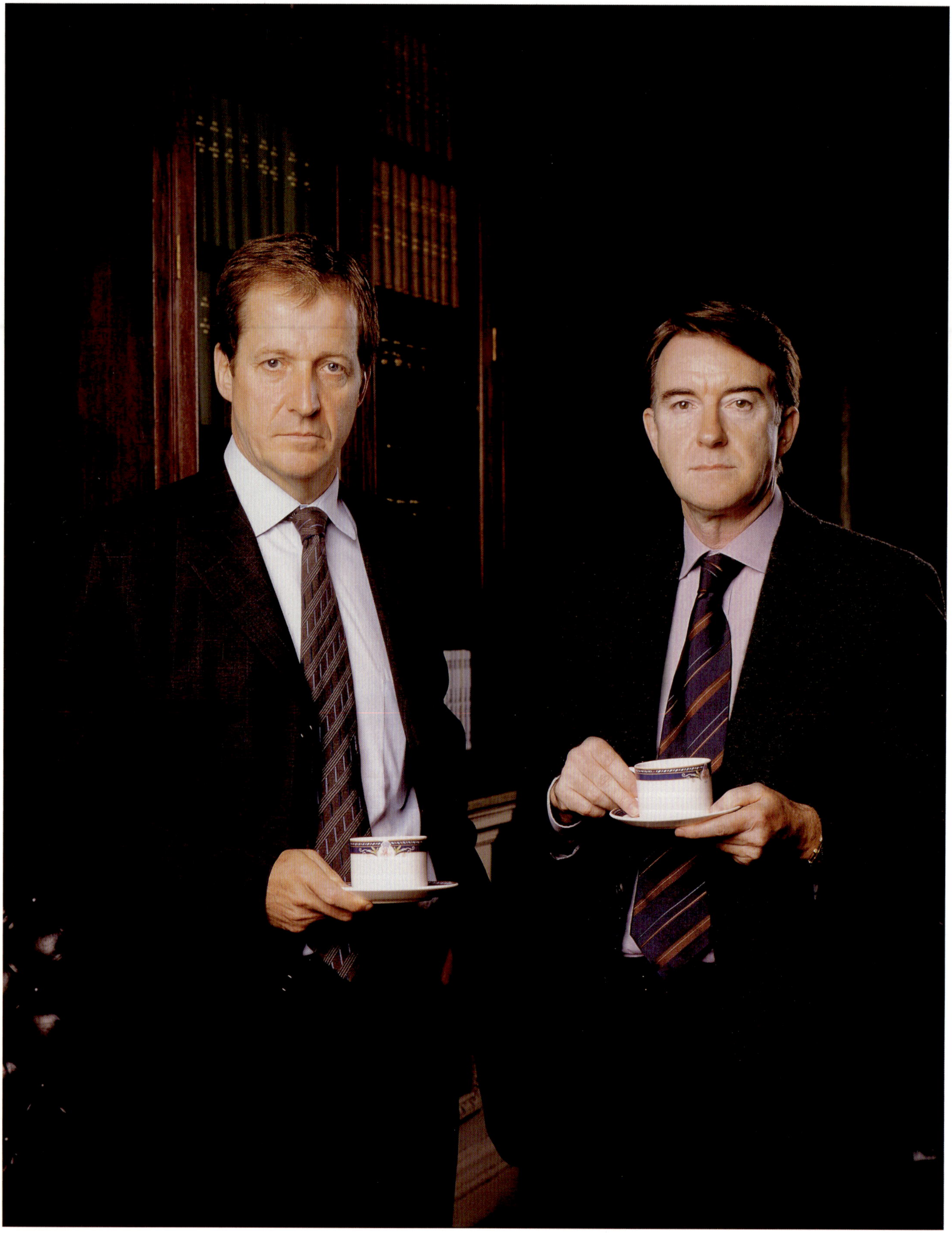

Harry Borden

Carol Vorderman
& Richard Whiteley
November 2004

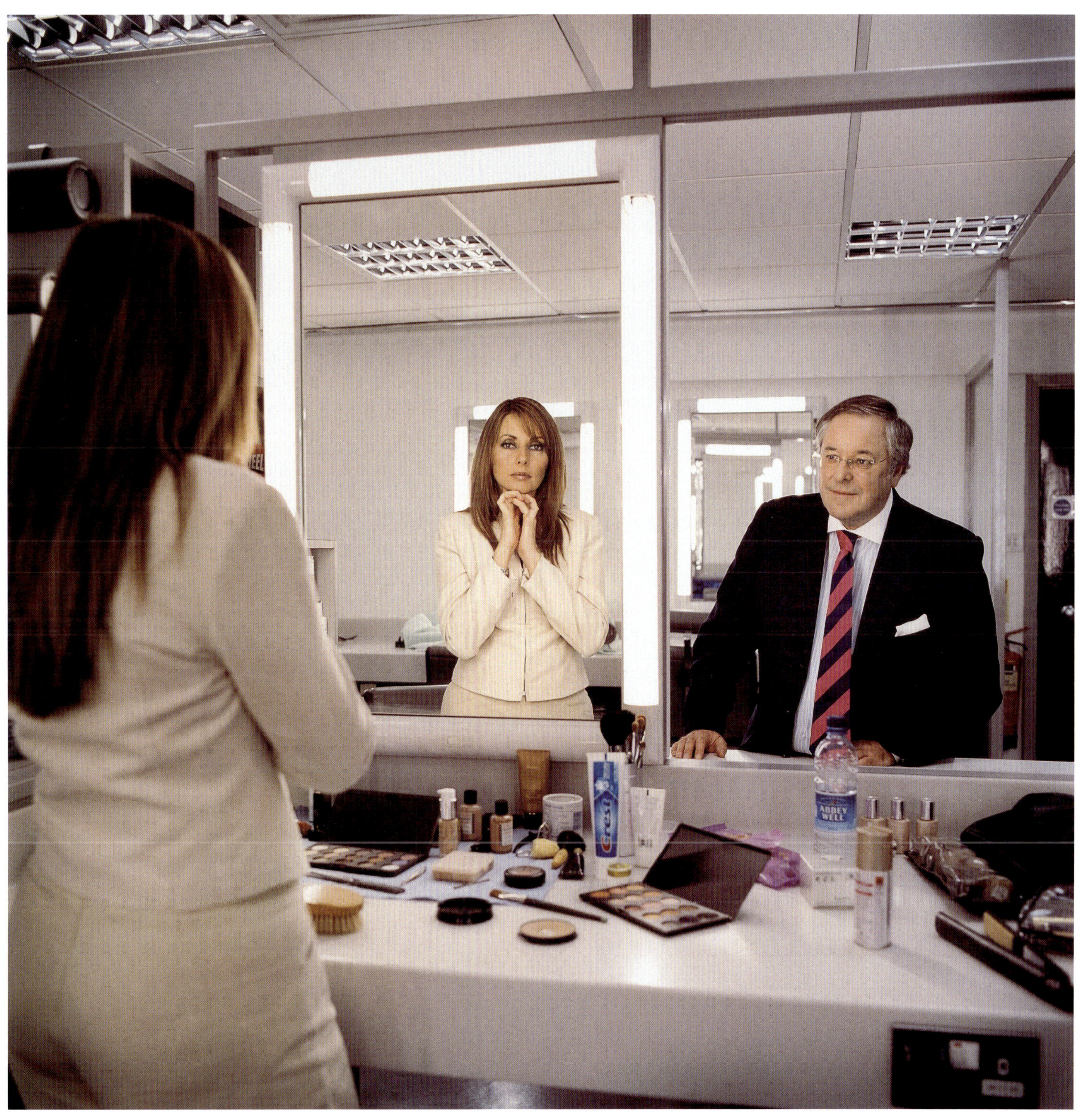

Oscar Arias

Soho Square,
South Bench
from the series
Soho Strangers
July 2004

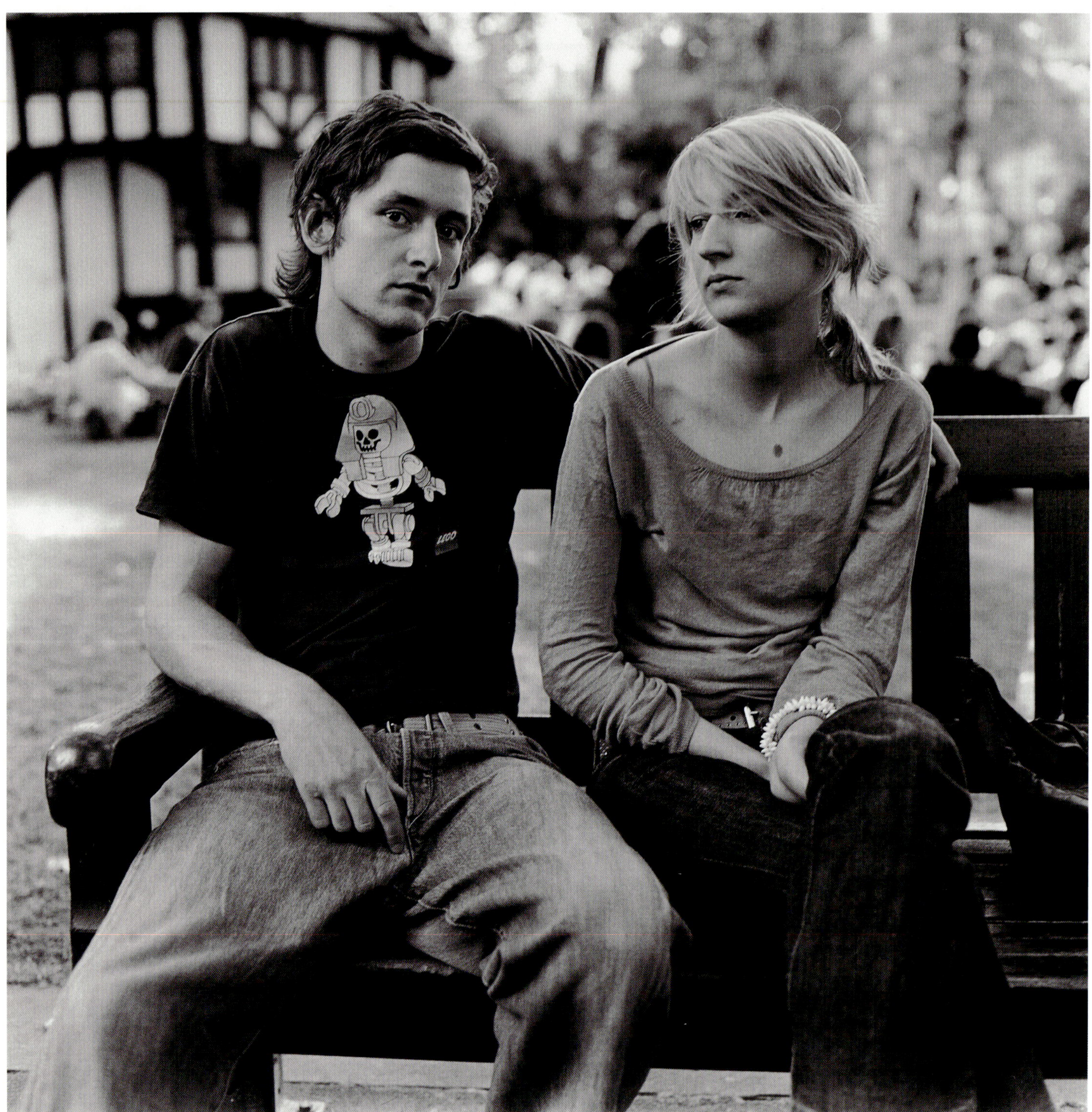

Simon
Obarzanek

Cranbourne
Girl Freckles
from the series
123 Faces
April 2005

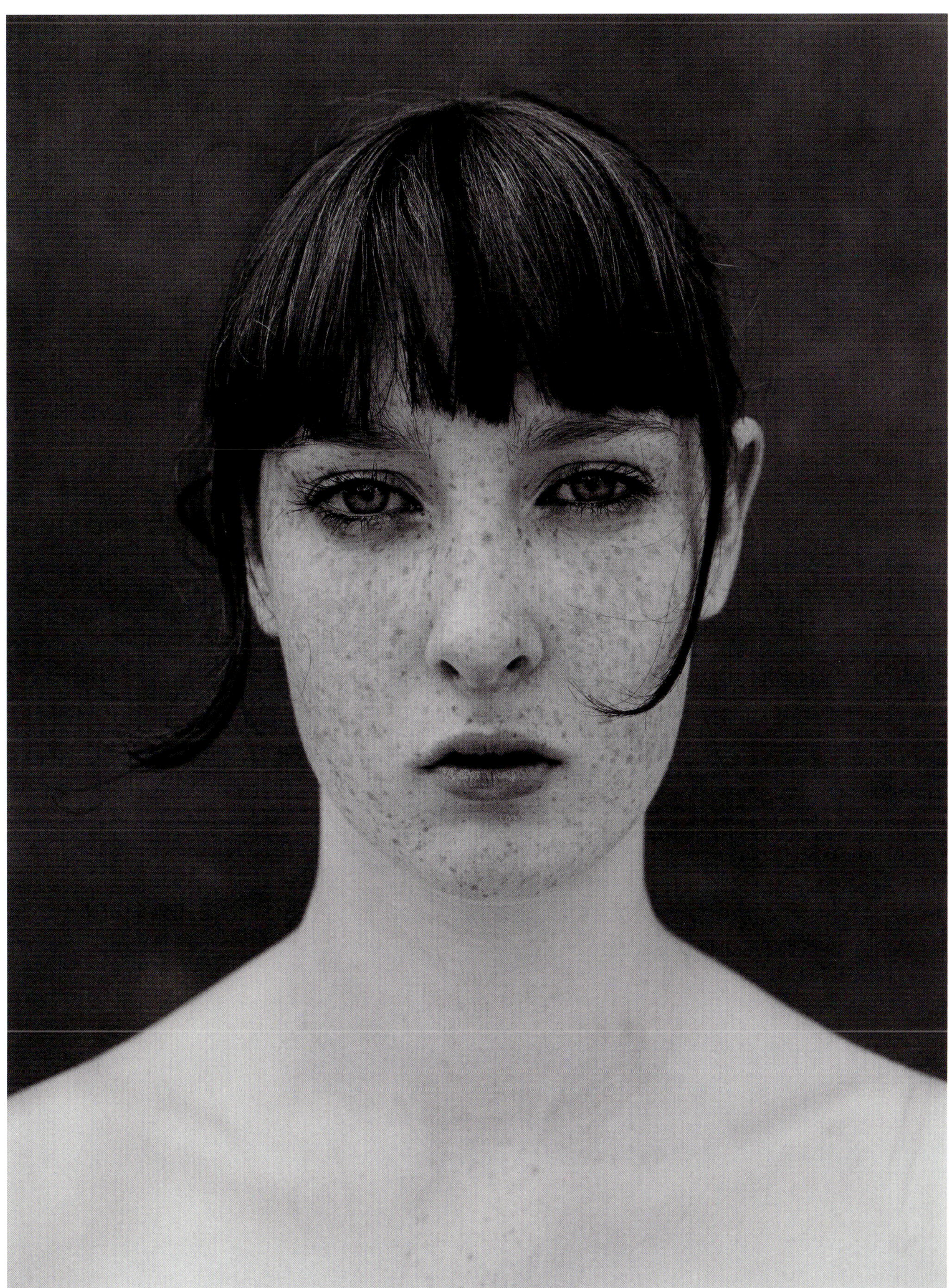

List of Exhibitors

A
Ambrosi, Maro 22
Ansett, Richard 24, 68
Arias, Oscar 70
Axelbank, David 48

B
Barry, Sheila 37
Blake, Paul 21
Borden, Harry 69
Bower, Ric
(Third Prize) 4, 10–11
Brooking, Paul 65
Broughton, Jo 56

C
Carnegie, Rory 63
Chelbin, Michal 31, 57
Craig, Tom 30
Crane, Charlie 41

D
Darby, Tara 35
Davies, Lottie 66
Deegan, Shane 18

E
Ebeling, Philipp
(Second Prize) 4, 8–9

F
Fullerton-Batten, Julia 33

G
Giles, Rick 49
Godwin, Giles 54

H
Hansen, Pål Christopher 38
Harris, Naomi 36
Hawkins, Matthew 32
Henderson, Shara
(First Prize) 4, 6–7
Hjorth, Karoline
(Deloitte Award) 4, 14–15
Hoyle, Matt 62

I
Illsley, Hannah 67

J
Jackling, Kate 25

K
Kander, Nadav 40
Kolker, Richard 28

L
Lane, Christopher 42
Laub, Gillian 34
Leahy, Clarissa 19
Lindner, Dirk 47

M
McKenzie, Duncan 53
MacPherson, Tim 44
Mankowitz, Gered 58
Meriau, Nadege 23
Modell, David 59
Molnar, Zsofia 52
Moore, Tara 60
Murray, Kelvin 64

N
Nelson, Zed 43

O
Obarzanek, Simon 71

P
Plews, Paul 50

R
Reed, Magnus
(Fourth Prize) 4, 12–13

S
Scheinmann, David 26
Slimm, Daniel 20
Stanley, Robin George 45
Stewart, David 51

T
Taylor, Steven 46
Thompson, Paul 39
Torgovnik, Jonathan 55

V
Vasan, Gandee 17

W
Want, Anton 29

Y
Yeats-Brown, James 61

Z
Zeschin, Elizabeth 27